296.9   035701

BURY EDUCATION COMMITTEE

PROJECT LOAN

BURY METRO LIBRARIES
000637872 X

Author:

Jacqueline Morley studied English at Oxford University. She has taught English and history and has a special interest in the history of everyday life. She has written historical fiction and non-fiction for children and is the author of the award-winning **An Egyptian Pyramid** in the *Inside Story* series.

Artist:

John James was born in London in 1959. He studied at Eastbourne College of Art and has specialised in historical reconstruction since leaving art school in 1982. He lives in Sussex with his wife and children.

Additional Artist: **Nick Hewetson**

Consultant:

Penina Efune studied Judaism in the Beth Rifka Seminary in New York and has since been a teacher of Jewish studies in the UK. She and her husband founded the Torah Academy Primary School in 1988 in Brighton, where she currently lives with her family.

Series creator:

David Salariya was born in Dundee, Scotland. In 1989, he established The Salariya Book Company. He has designed and created many new series for publishers in the UK and overseas. He lives in Brighton with his wife, the illustrator Shirley Willis, and their son Jonathan.

Editor: **Karen Barker Smith**

Assistant Editor: **Stephanie Cole**

© The Salariya Book Company Limited MMI
All rights reserved. No part of this book may be reproduced, stored in a retrieval system or transmitted in any form or by any means, electronic, mechanical, photocopying, recording, or otherwise, without the written permission of the copyright owner.

Published in Great Britain in 2003 by
Book House, an imprint of
The Salariya Book Company Ltd
25 Marlborough Place, Brighton BN1 1UB

Visit the Salariya Book Company at:
www.salariya.com
www.book-house.co.uk

A catalogue record for this book is available
from the British library

ISBN 1 904194 69 9

Printed and bound in Belgium.
Printed on paper from sustainable forests.

CONTENTS

The Temple at Jerusalem	6
Worship in high places	8
The tabernacle	10
Building the Temple	12
The Temple completed	14
The fall of Jerusalem	16
Exile in Babylon	18
Rebuilding the Temple	20
Greek influence	22
Revolt of the Maccabees	24
Roman Jerusalem	26
Herod's Temple	28
Priests and Levites	30
The Day of Atonement	32
Pilgrimage festivals	34
The final destruction	36
After the Temple	38
The Temple site today	40
Timespan	42
Glossary	44
Index	45

MAGNIFICATIONS

The Temple at Jerusalem

PROJECT LOAN

Written by
Jacqueline Morley

Series created by
David Salariya

Illustrated by
John James

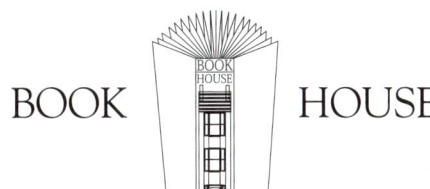

The Temple at Jerusalem

TEMPLES HAVE BEEN BUILT as houses for gods for thousands of years. About 3,000 years ago, the Jews built a temple in Jerusalem to their God. This building was particularly special in Jewish life because, unlike other peoples of that time, the Jews worshipped only one God and had only one Temple. It was the place where they felt closest to their God. The Temple at Jerusalem was destroyed nearly 2,000 years ago but the Jews still mourn its loss. It was much more to them than a house for a god, for they had come to realise that the creator of all things could not be contained in a house. It was the symbol of God's presence among the Jewish people and of his blessing of their nation.

The story of the Temple covers many centuries and involves several European and eastern-Mediterranean lands. This map (right) shows the most important of these.

To Jews today, the vanished Temple is the spiritual home that the Messiah will restore. For Christians, it is a symbol of God's Heavenly City. Each age has had its idea of what the original Temple looked like. Below is a medieval version.

This map (left) shows Jerusalem and its surroundings. Not all the places marked existed at the same time and some changed their names. Jerusalem is in the region known in biblical times as Canaan. Its Roman name was Palestine.

A 15th-century artist imagined a temple interior with twisted columns (left) which were widely supposed to have been a feature of the Temple. Some similar columns existed in St. Peter's church in Rome in medieval times that were mistakenly believed to have come from the Temple.

In the 15th century, people thought the Temple Mount would have looked like a medieval city ringed with walls and towers (right). At its heart is a circular Temple.

In the 16th century, the Temple was imagined as a building of Renaissance design, with sculpted figures decorating its facade (below right).

This 18th-century picture of the Temple courtyard (left) was based on biblical description. However, the detail on the items shown is invented.

A 17th-century vision of the Temple sets it on a platform high above Jerusalem (below). This version has some striking similarities with that produced by modern research (see picture of Temple on pages 26-27).

7

THE ORIGIN OF THE ISRAELITES

WORSHIP IN HIGH PLACES

Abraham's family had travelled from the city of Ur in Mesopotamia to the area that is south Turkey today. They settled in Haran.

At God's command, Abraham led his people south from Haran into Canaan (a region that includes modern Israel). This was the land God had promised them.

Abraham's family thrived in Canaan. It is said that his grandson Jacob wrestled with an angel, earning him the name Israel (Champion of God).

Jacob had twelve sons whose descendants formed twelve tribes known as the Israelites, in memory of Jacob's God-given name. Jacob's favourite son was Joseph, the youngest. The elder brothers were jealous and hated Joseph.

FROM THE BEGINNING of their history, the Jewish people have had an overwhelming sense of the presence of God in their lives. The Bible tells how long, long ago (perhaps around 2,000 BC) a man called Abraham, who was the ancestor of the Jews, heard God speaking to him directly. God promised to protect Abraham's people and to lead them to a fruitful land that would be theirs forever, if they obeyed his laws. Abraham was the leader of a tribe of wandering herdsmen and, in that distant time, each tribe had its own god. However, Abraham's people believed in an invisible God who was the Creator of the entire universe.

Abraham's people lived in tents (right) as they had to move about in search of grazing land for their herds. Their sheep and goats provided them with life's essentials – food and clothing.

THE STORY OF JOSEPH

Joseph's brothers planned to kill him. They threw him into a pit, but seeing some travelling merchants they decided to sell him instead.

The merchants took Joseph to Egypt, a rich land ruled by a mighty king, the Pharaoh. They sold him to a royal official and Joseph became a trusted steward. However, through no fault of his own, Joseph was thrown into prison. The Pharaoh freed Joseph because he was able to interpret a dream that the king had had.

Joseph warned the Pharaoh that his dream foretold famine and he advised him to stockpile wheat. The Pharaoh made Joseph his chief minister.

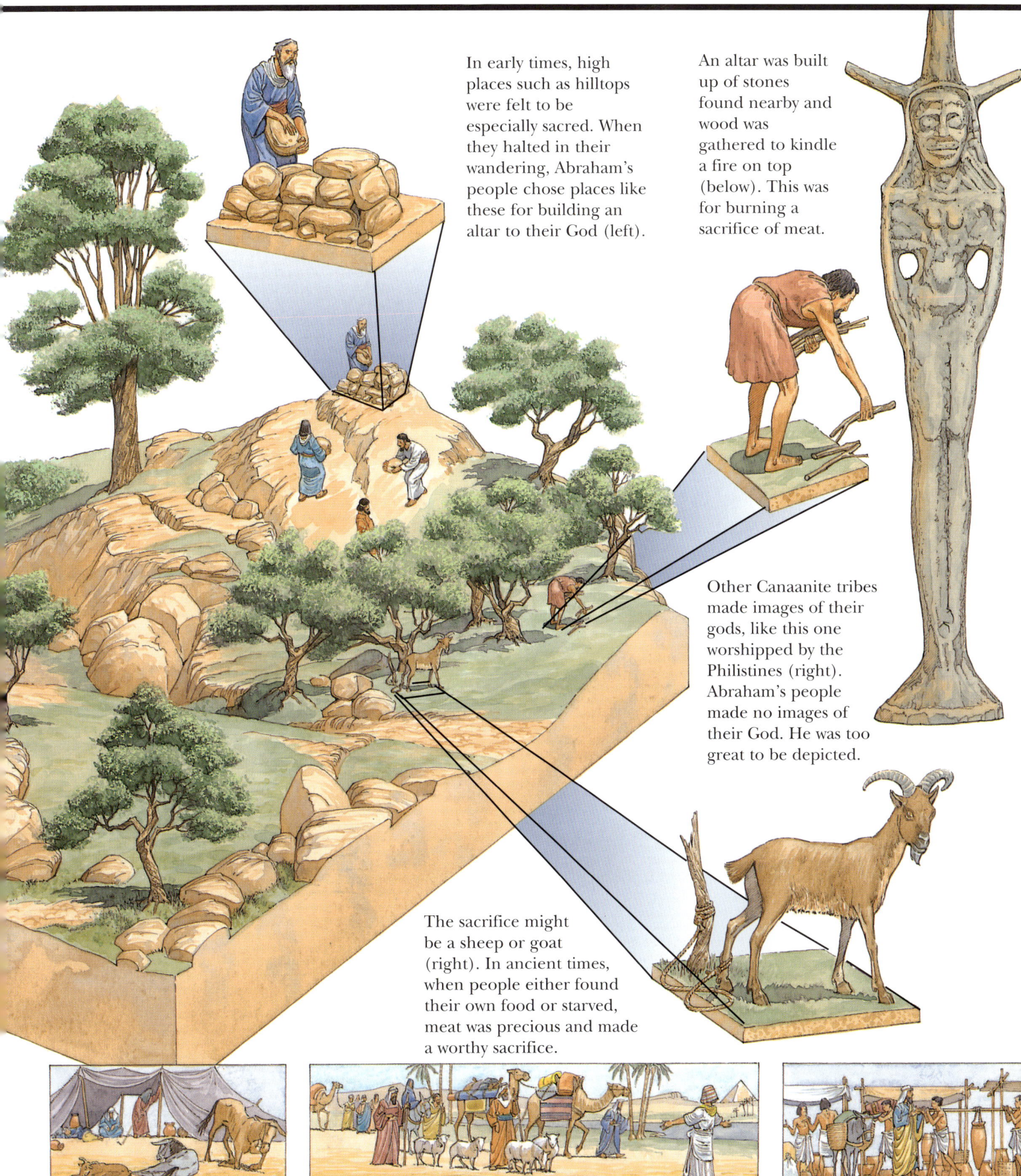

In early times, high places such as hilltops were felt to be especially sacred. When they halted in their wandering, Abraham's people chose places like these for building an altar to their God (left).

An altar was built up of stones found nearby and wood was gathered to kindle a fire on top (below). This was for burning a sacrifice of meat.

Other Canaanite tribes made images of their gods, like this one worshipped by the Philistines (right). Abraham's people made no images of their God. He was too great to be depicted.

The sacrifice might be a sheep or goat (right). In ancient times, when people either found their own food or starved, meat was precious and made a worthy sacrifice.

When the famine came, there was no food in Canaan for Jacob's people or their beasts. However, the Egyptians had wheat, so Jacob sent his ten eldest sons to Egypt to buy some.

The brothers were overawed by the Egyptian minister who was organising the sale of wheat, not recognising their brother Joseph. When at last Joseph told them who he was, the brothers were reconciled. Joseph urged his brothers to fetch their ageing father so that they could all live together. Jacob came to Egypt to be reunited with his long-lost son.

In this way, the Israelites came to live in Egypt. They made a good living for themselves and had many children so that, in time, they settled throughout the land.

ESCAPE FROM EGYPT

Though welcome in Egypt at first, the Israelites were later enslaved as brick-makers for the pharaohs' vast building projects.

Moses and his brother Aaron begged the Pharaoh to free the Israelites and let them return to Canaan, but he would not let them go.

The Bible tells how God sent plagues to punish the Egyptians and helped the Israelites to escape when the Egyptian army was pursuing them.

The Israelites went east into the desert. God showed them the route, going ahead in the form of a pillar of cloud by day and a pillar of fire by night.

THE TABERNACLE

THE BIBLE CONTINUES with the story of the Israelites' return to Canaan. They were led from Egypt through the Sinai desert by Moses, the first of the great Jewish prophets. God called Moses to receive the Ten Commandments, the rules of conduct which gave the Jewish faith its strong sense of right and wrong. Through Moses, God also told the Israelites to build a tabernacle (a tent) in which he would dwell among them.

Christian version of the tabernacle

The biblical book of *Shemot* (Exodus) gives an exact description of the tabernacle, its courtyard and its contents. Jews and Christians interpret some details slightly differently. Inset is the Christian version.

Animals were sacrificed on the 'altar of burnt offerings' in the outer court. These animals had to be male and without imperfections (right).

THE COVENANT AND THE ARK

When the Israelites were camped by Mount Sinai, there was thunder and lightning and God spoke. He called Moses to the top of the mountain.

Moses was away on the mountain for 40 days according to the Bible. The Israelites began to fear that he would not return and that their God had abandoned them. Some of them made an image of a calf out of gold and worshipped that instead. They offered it sacrifices and danced around it.

When Moses found his people dancing around an idol, he was so angry that he broke the two stone tablets given to him by God, listing God's laws and his Covenant.

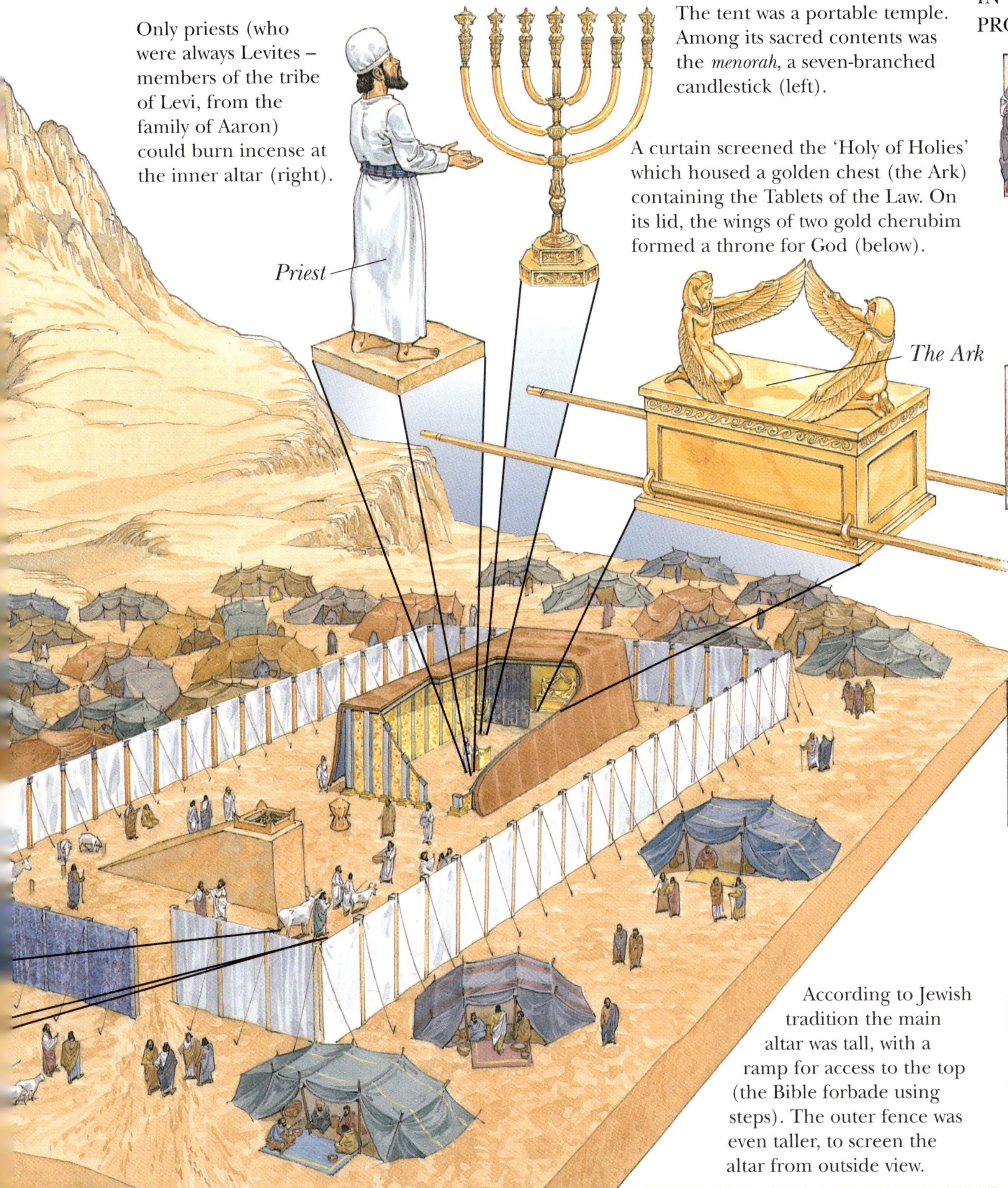

IN THE PROMISED LAND

The menorah

Only priests (who were always Levites – members of the tribe of Levi, from the family of Aaron) could burn incense at the inner altar (right).

The tent was a portable temple. Among its sacred contents was the *menorah*, a seven-branched candlestick (left).

A curtain screened the 'Holy of Holies' which housed a golden chest (the Ark) containing the Tablets of the Law. On its lid, the wings of two gold cherubim formed a throne for God (below).

Priest

The Ark

According to Jewish tradition the main altar was tall, with a ramp for access to the top (the Bible forbade using steps). The outer fence was even taller, to screen the altar from outside view.

The Israelites settled in Canaan around 1200 BC. At first, the tribes had no king. In a crisis they relied on a judge or prophet stepping forward.

The Israelites had to fight many enemies in Canaan. They took the Ark with them into battle, believing it would bring them victory.

The Israelite tribes of northern Canaan asked the prophet Samuel to choose a king. He anointed the warrior Saul as the king of Israel.

Saul ruled for 40 years. After Saul's death, his son-in-law David was anointed king of both Judah and Israel.

God agreed to protect his people if they promised to worship only him. They brought offerings of gold, silver, timber and hides to build a home for two new 'Tablets of the Law'.

God gave Moses instructions for building the tabernacle that was to house the Ark of the Covenant, containing the Tablets of the Law. Everybody helped to make it. The women spun thread to weave its curtains, men cut posts to support it and metalworkers ornamented it with gold and silver.

When the Israelites set off again on their way to Canaan, they took the tabernacle apart and carried the Ark and its coverings with the greatest care.

THE CITY OF DAVID

David captured Jerusalem from the Jebusites. It was then a small city on the ridge of a hill.

David had increased the Israelites' territory and he wanted a capital that reflected his power. He enlarged the city and extended its walls.

It is said David angered God, who spread plague in the land. But he halted his plague-bearing angel on a hill above Jerusalem and spared the city.

This hilltop was then seen as holy and as a fitting site for the Ark's home. David bought the site from its Jebusite owner who had used it as a threshing floor.

Building the Temple

UP TO THIS POINT the story of the Jews relies on biblical traditions, but from the time of King David there is historical evidence as well. Around 1,000 BC David captured the city of Jerusalem and made it his capital. This was the obvious home for the Israelites' most precious possession, the Ark. David had it brought there and planned to build a temple to house it, but the scheme was not carried out until the reign of his son, Solomon. Due to David's skill as a warrior, Solomon inherited a rich and powerful empire. He could afford to build a temple worthy to be God's house on Earth.

Chief bronzesmith

The vast water-storage basin was cast in bronze in several pieces. Installing it was a huge task overseen by the chief bronzesmith (left).

Pine and cedar wood (below) had to be imported from Lebanon because Israel had no suitable forests. Solomon paid for it with wheat and oil.

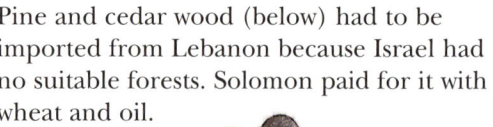

Overseer

Overseers kept an eye on the progress and standard of work (left).

THE ARK ENTERS JERUSALEM

David ordered the Ark, which had been housed in the west of his kingdom, to be taken to Jerusalem.

Crowds lined the streets to celebrate the Ark's entry into Jerusalem. It was carried by white-robed Levites, to the sounds of trumpets, harps and cymbals, and to singing and shouts of joy. Dressed in a priestly tunic, King David leapt and danced before the Ark to express his gladness and to honour God. The Ark was taken through the city to a special tent.

The Ark was carried with great ceremony into the tent which was its home until a temple could be built for it.

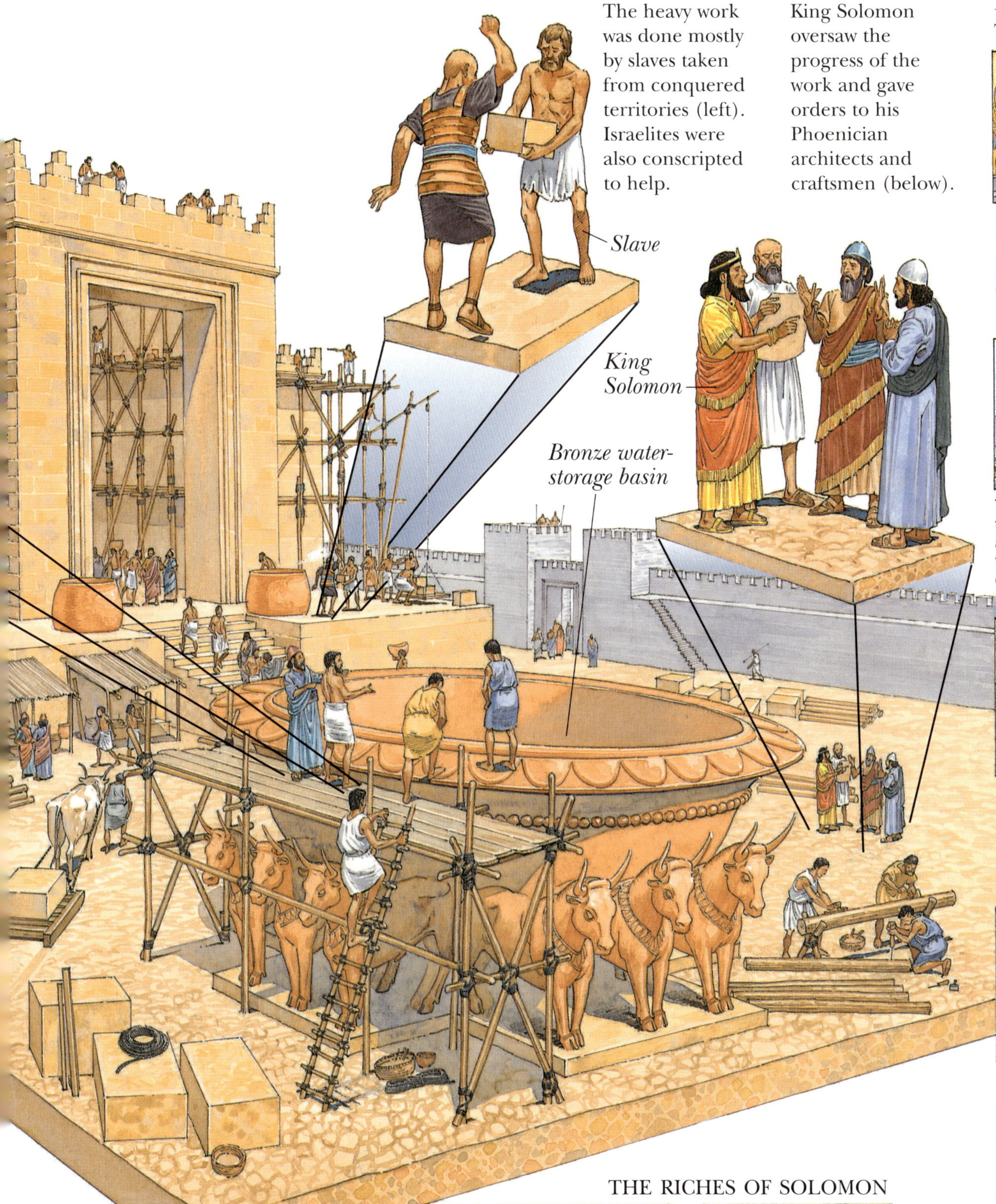

The heavy work was done mostly by slaves taken from conquered territories (left). Israelites were also conscripted to help.

King Solomon oversaw the progress of the work and gave orders to his Phoenician architects and craftsmen (below).

Slave

King Solomon

Bronze water-storage basin

BUILDING THE TEMPLE

Solomon's envoy asked King Hiram to supply Phoenician craftsmen to help build the Temple. They had many skills the Israelites lacked.

Timber from Hiram's forests was floated south along the coast from Tyre to Joppa and taken overland to Jerusalem.

According to the Bible, all stone was shaped at the quarry so that the peace of the Temple was not disturbed by the din of axes and hammers.

Copper, needed to make the bronze used in the Temple, was mined and smelted at the royal copper works near the Red Sea.

THE RICHES OF SOLOMON

David's son, Solomon, ruled for 40 prosperous years. He was famous for his wealth and for the wisdom of his judgments.

King Solomon made alliances with neighbouring countries in order to increase the foreign trade that made Israel rich. Sometimes he cemented the alliance by marrying the ruler's daughter – Solomon had many wives and even married an Egyptian princess.

With the help of his close ally, the Phoenician King Hiram of Tyre, Solomon built a fleet and imported gold via the Red Sea.

The bronze-casting was done in the Jordan valley. Finished pieces were then taken overland to Jerusalem.

THE TEMPLE COMPLETED

BY THE ELEVENTH year of Solomon's reign (probably 952 BC) the temple was finished. Though not a big building, it was famed for its magnificence. Its walls, ceiling and contents were all made of gold or gold-inlaid. Its exact appearance is not known. This drawing (right) is based on biblical and archaeological evidence. The dwelling place of God was so holy that only priests were allowed to enter. As they went from the courtyard through the *ulam* (porch) and into the *hekal* (holy place) they were treading on increasingly sacred ground, leading to the *devir* (holy of holies) which only the high priest could enter.

Attendant priests brought portions of the sacrifice to the altar (right). Strict rules governed which animals could be sacrificed and which parts burned. According to the Bible, God gave these rules to Moses.

The priests' chief duty was to offer daily sacrifices on the altar in the courtyard (right). Ordinary Israelites watched the ceremonies but could not touch the altar.

Attendant priest

Altar

JERUSALEM BECOMES A HOLY SITE

At the Temple's dedication ceremony, priests carried the Ark of the Covenant in a solemn procession from the tent provided by David to its final home. It was placed in the Holy of Holies, under the wings of the cherubim.

With the Ark safely installed, King Solomon turned to bless the congregation in the courtyard. He raised his arms to give thanks to God: "God of Israel, there is no God like thee, in heaven above or on earth beneath."

In his speech to the people, Solomon posed the question: how could a God who was everywhere be contained in the Temple? But God said, "My name shall be there." The Temple was a place of special access to him.

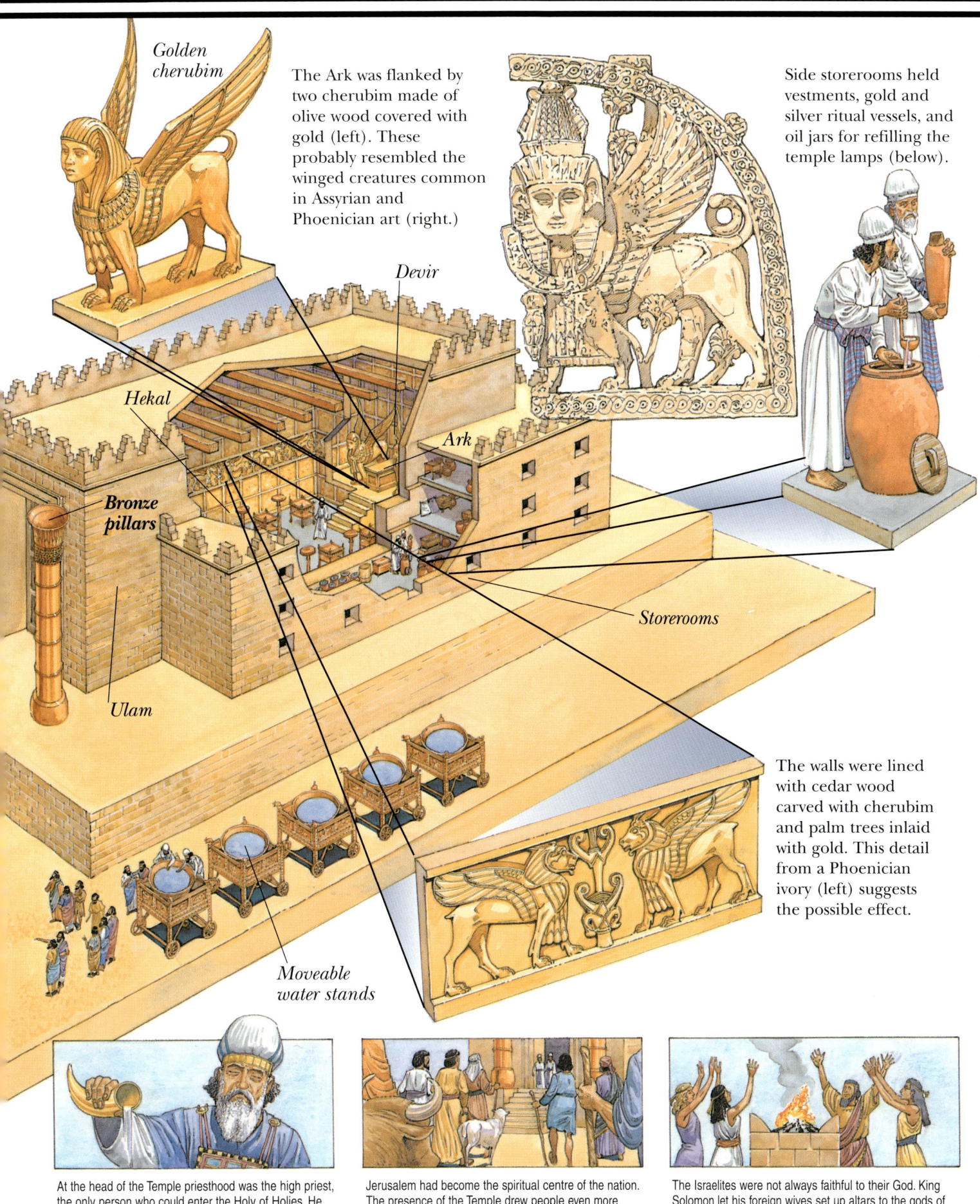

THE RISE OF ASSYRIA

The Assyrians began their expansion westward in 745 BC, when Tiglath-Pileser, a ruthless empire-builder, became their king.

To appease the Assyrians, Judah's King Ahaz had the Temple's great basin dismantled in 730 BC. He sent the bronze bullocks as tribute payment.

The Assyrians destroyed the kingdom of Israel. Twenty-seven thousand Israelites were led away and replaced by foreign settlers.

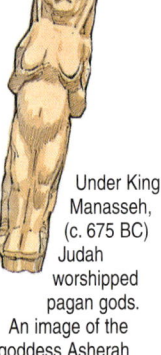

Under King Manasseh, (c. 675 BC) Judah worshipped pagan gods. An image of the goddess Asherah was put in the Temple itself. Prophets warned the Jews repeatedly that God would punish idol worship. Future events seemed to prove them right.

THE FALL OF JERUSALEM

THE MISRULE OF SOLOMON'S SON Rehoboam split his realm apart. For two centuries it was again two kingdoms, Israel and Judah. These were no match for a new enemy, the warlike Assyrians, who conquered Israel in 722 BC and deported its people. What became of them no one knows. Only the Israelites of Judah survived, to become known as the Jews. Judah's attempts to keep its independence were doomed. In 586 BC the Babylonians seized Jerusalem, destroyed the Temple and led many of the Jews captive to Babylon.

Jewish defender

The Jews bravely defended their city (above), hurling torches and stones and toppling ladders.

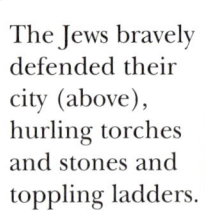

Assyrians had a reputation for cruelty. This relief (left) shows Assyrians punishing their enemies by impaling them alive on stakes.

This relief (right) shows the Assyrian warrior king, Tiglath-Pileser III. He made Assyria feared far and wide.

Tiglath-Pileser III

DISCOVERING THE TORAH SCROLL

King Josiah of Judah heeded the prophets' warning. He rejected pagan worship and in c. 630 BC restored the dilapidated 300-year old Temple.

During the restoration, a priest found a scroll recording the laws God gave Moses and God's covenant to protect his people while they obeyed them.

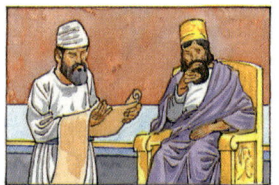

The scroll contained the Torah. When it was read to Josiah, he was shocked to realize how neglectful of God's laws the Jews had become.

Josiah ordered a religious purge and strict obedience to God's laws. All pagan priests were killed and their altars broken and beaten to powder.

Nebuchadnezzar, King of Babylon, led the disciplined Babylonian army (right). His charioteers were more formidable than anything the Jews could muster.

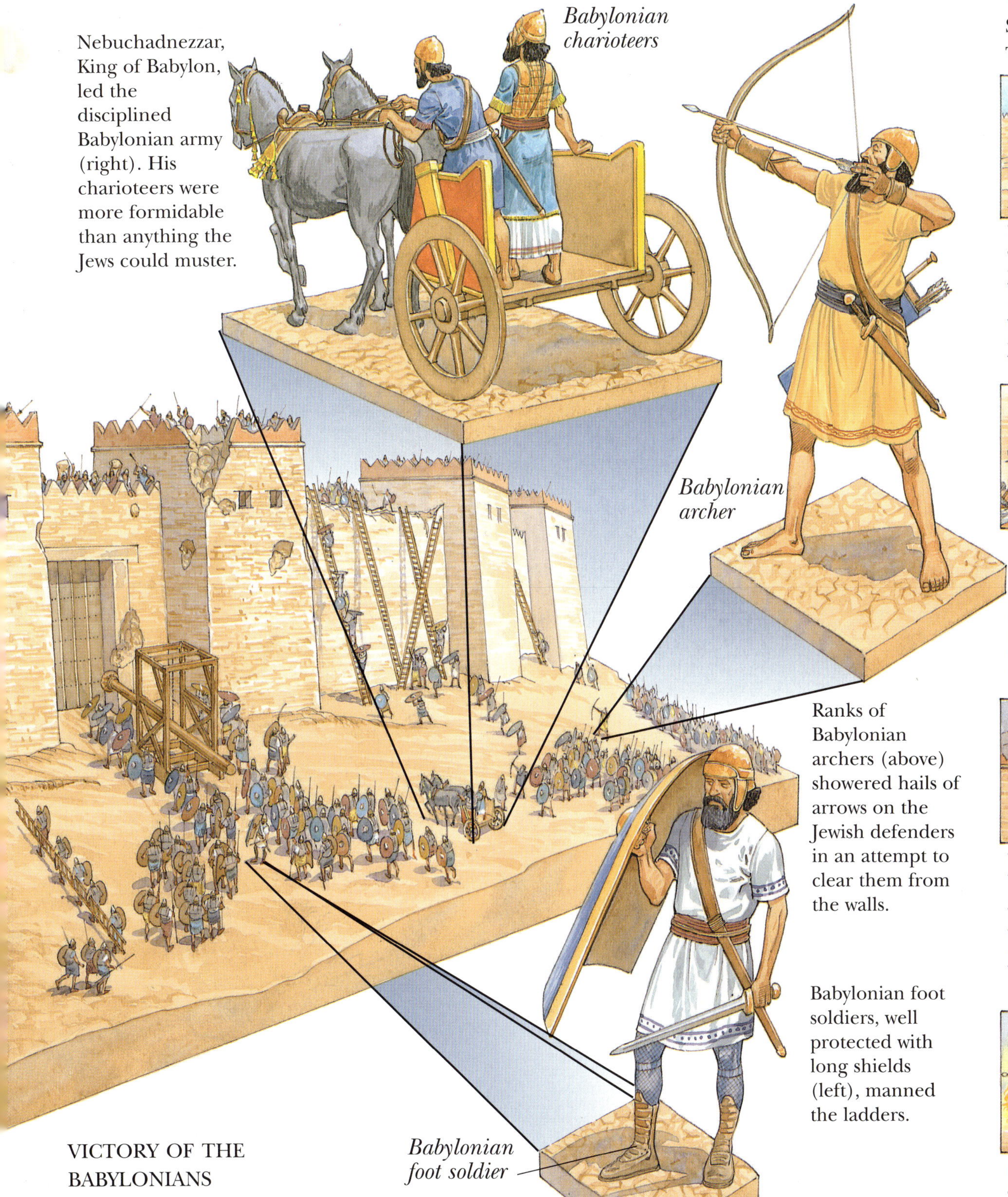

Babylonian charioteers

Babylonian archer

Ranks of Babylonian archers (above) showered hails of arrows on the Jewish defenders in an attempt to clear them from the walls.

Babylonian foot soldiers, well protected with long shields (left), manned the ladders.

Babylonian foot soldier

THE END OF SOLOMON'S TEMPLE

When the conquered Jerusalem rebelled against its new masters, the Babylonians returned and besieged the city for 18 months. In 586 BC they breached the city wall.

Soldiers broke in, looting and destroying. They smashed the twin bronze pillars of the Temple and carted them off for their scrap value.

The Babylonians set fire to the Temple, the palace and the houses. They destroyed the city walls and reduced much of Jerusalem to rubble.

Now it was the turn of Jerusalem's workers to be led away to Babylon. Only very poor labourers, too unimportant to move, were left in the city.

VICTORY OF THE BABYLONIANS

Even the Assyrians met their match eventually. In 612 BC, the Babylonians sacked their capital, Ninevah, and the Assyrian Empire crumbled.

In 597 BC the Babylonians took Jerusalem. The king surrendered without a fight. The Temple was plundered and its treasures stolen.

The Babylonians installed a puppet ruler in Jerusalem and led the captive king and all Judah's nobles and skilled workers to Babylon.

The prophet Jeremiah warned the people of Jerusalem that worse would follow unless they did more to deserve God's protection.

Exile in Babylon

Mourning for Jerusalem

MANY JEWS had thought that Jerusalem, God's home, could never fall. The destruction of the city seemed to bring their world to an end. However, in their years of exile, the Jews came to a new understanding of God's promise to protect them. If they followed his laws faithfully, he would be with them wherever they were. The study and understanding of the Torah, or Law, became central to the Jewish faith. Nonetheless, they mourned the lost Temple, without which they were unable to offer sacrifices to express their faith.

The people left in Judah gathered twice-yearly in the deserted Jerusalem to mourn their lost city. They sang laments among its ruins.

The Jews in Babylon were not badly treated. They were allowed to trade and in time some even became court officials.

In place of worship in the Temple, the exiles kept their faith alive by studying the Jewish holy writings and discussing their meaning together.

The lost Temple was still the focus of Jewish worship. Whenever the exiles prayed, they stretched their hands towards Jerusalem.

Ezekiel

The Magnificence of Babylon

At their first sight of Babylon, the Jews gazed in amazement. It was the greatest city of the Near East. Its triple walls stretched over 16 kilometres to protect the city and were ringed by a wide and busy canal. The river Euphrates, the trade route that had made Babylon so rich, ran through the centre of the city.

The buildings of Babylon were astonishing. A seven-tiered ziggurat towered over the city's old quarter. Lush gardens, constantly irrigated and artfully designed to spill down over artificial terraces, adorned the magnificent new district created by the king.

The visionary Temple

The prophet Ezekiel comforted the exiled Jews by telling of a vision he had had. He had been transported to Jerusalem and was shown a glorious new Temple. This was a message of hope: the Temple would be rebuilt.

In his vision, Ezekiel saw a man of bronze with a measuring rod and measuring line in his hands (above). He guided Ezekiel through the chambers of the visionary Temple and gave him the measurements of all its parts.

Ezekiel was shown a rivulet rising from the Temple that swelled into a mighty river flowing through the land. Its banks were lined with trees laden with fruit (left) and multitudes of fish filled its waters (above). These were the Waters of Life, springing from God to nourish his people.

As well as being the heart of a political empire, Babylon was also the centre of worship to the most important Mesopotamian god, Marduk. On festival days, the god's statue was paraded along the processional avenue leading to the city's Ishtar Gate. The king accompanied the idol in his chariot.

The Jews turned in horror from such scenes. The idea of worshipping idols was hateful to them – God was far too great to be portrayed by humans. Jewish philosophers had developed the idea that there was only one God, who made all things. Marduk did not really exist.

THE RETURN TO JERUSALEM

In a series of brilliant campaigns, King Cyrus of Persia made himself master of the whole of the Near East, up to the borders of India.

Cyrus treated the Jews fairly. He ordered the return of all the gold and silver vessels that Nebuchadnezzar had seized from the Temple.

The first thing the Jews did upon returning to the ruins of Jerusalem was to rebuild the great altar, so they could offer sacrifices again.

Hunger discouraged people from building. The prophet Haggai said their priorities were wrong. If they finished the Temple the famine would end.

The foundations of the second Temple were finished in 520 BC. Old people who had seen the glory of Solomon's Temple wept at the contrast (below).

At the ceremony of rededication priests processed into the sacred area, singing songs, clashing cymbals and dancing with joy (right).

The High Priest, dressed in his ceremonial robe, led the procession and made the thanksgiving sacrifice.

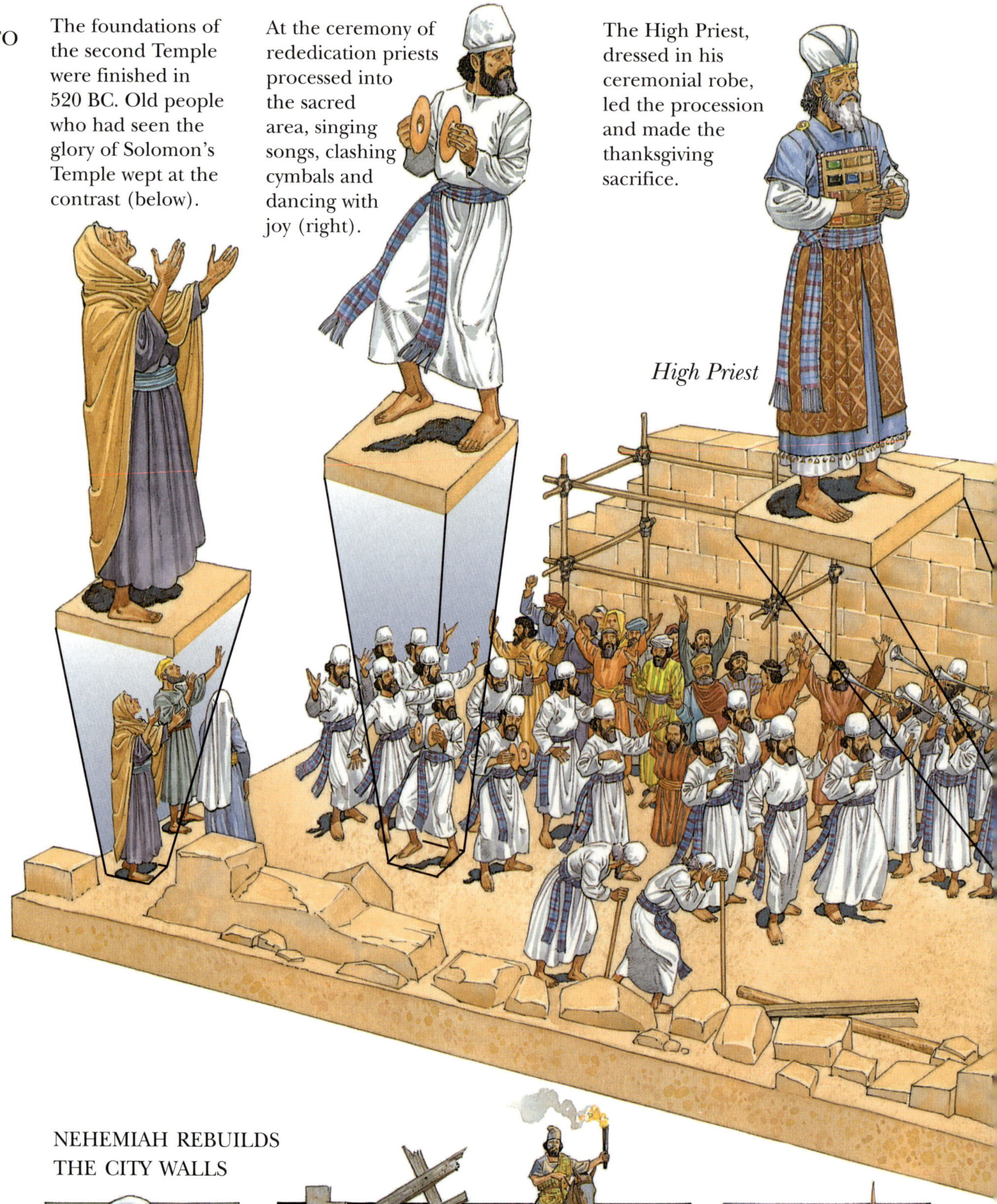

High Priest

NEHEMIAH REBUILDS THE CITY WALLS

The Persian king had a Jewish cupbearer called Nehemiah. When he heard of his peoples' suffering in Jerusalem he was grief-stricken.

Nehemiah begged the king to let him go to Judah to help rebuild Jerusalem. The king appointed him governor and in c. 445 BC he arrived and explored the city by night. He was dismayed to find the walls nothing but fallen stone and their gates charred wood.

Nehemiah got people working at once on rebuilding the city walls. Each worker kept a weapon near at hand for fear of foreign attackers.

Rebuilding the Temple

WHEN THE PERSIANS conquered Babylon in 539 BC, King Cyrus, its new ruler, gave the Jews permission to return to Jerusalem and rebuild their Temple. At first, things went badly for the homecoming Jews. They struggled to grow food and make homes for themselves in the ruined city. Crops failed and they went hungry. Their neighbours (descendants of the settlers brought in by the Assyrians) were hostile and tried to get them into trouble with the Persians. Rebuilding was going at a snail's pace when the prophet Haggai gave the people new strength and inspired them to a great communal effort. By 515 BC Jerusalem had its Temple again.

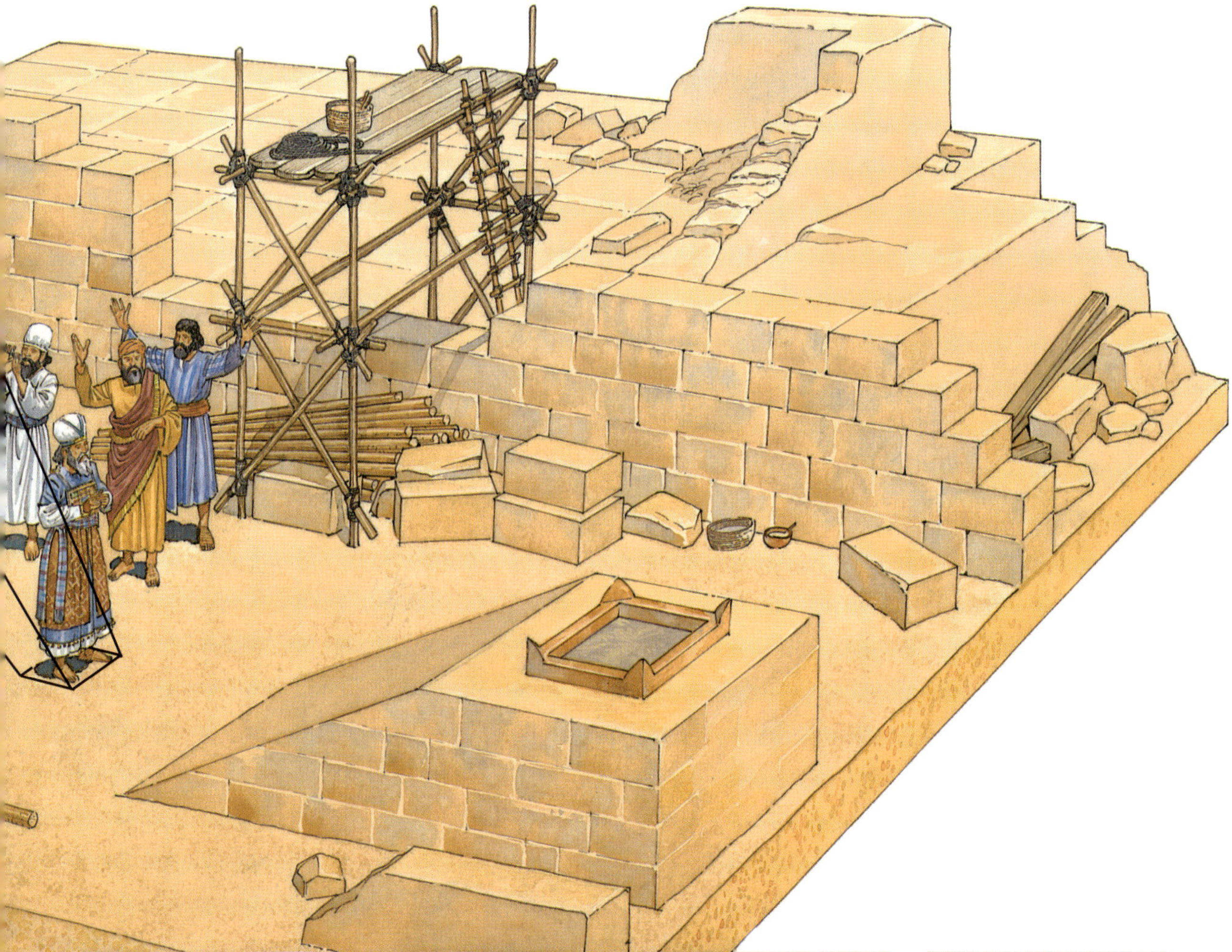

EZRA AND THE LAW

When the prophet Ezra went from Persia to Jerusalem in 398 BC, he wept in the streets at the sight of people's sinful behaviour.

Ezra had made a close study of the Torah. He called people together and read and explained it to them.

Among the laws that people neglected was the one that they should live in huts made of branches during the festival of *Sukkot*.

Ezra convinced the people that they must live according to the Torah. Foreign wives – a bad influence – had to be sent away.

Many of the returned Jews farmed in Judah. To revitalise Jerusalem, Nehemiah made one man in ten, chosen by drawing lots, move to the city.

In September 445 BC the new walls were dedicated. Priests and choristers formed two huge choirs that went in procession round the walls in opposite directions, singing psalms and sounding silver trumpets. Then they met and filed together into the Temple courtyard. The music and shouts of rejoicing could be heard for miles around.

Slowly, the city of Jerusalem was rebuilt. The new Temple was similar in size and design to Solomon's Temple but without its lavish decoration.

THE RISE OF THE EGYPTIAN GREEKS

GREEK INFLUENCE

FOR TWO CENTURIES, the Jews lived in strict obedience to the laws reintroduced by Ezra. The defeat of the Persians by Alexander the Great in 333 BC brought a disturbing new influence into their lives – the culture of ancient Greece. Some Jews, especially the more wealthy among them, came to admire Greek art, philosophy and poetry and tried to combine a Greek lifestyle with Jewish beliefs. Others distrusted the Greek habit of questioning even the most sacred things. Under the influence of pro-Greek high priests, Greek educational methods were adopted. A *gymnasion*, where Jewish youths practised Greek sports naked, in the Greek manner, was opened near the Temple. Many older Jews were outraged by such indecency.

When King Darius II was defeated by Alexander the Great of Macedonia (northern Greece), the Persian Empire crumbled.

When Alexander died suddenly in 323 BC, his quarrelling generals, Ptolemy and Seleucus, split the Greek Empire in two.

Ptolemy's descendants ruled Egypt; Seleucus' held Mesopotamia. They fought over the land in between, which included Judea (Judah).

Many Jews were moved to Alexandria in Greek Egypt. Their descendants became so influenced by Greek culture that they needed to make a Greek translation of the Torah.

Jewish intellectuals met at the *gymnasion* to exchange ideas (above). This followed ancient Greek tradition.

Young men trained in the central court (right), which was surrounded by halls for indoor practice and for the study of philosophy.

UNDER THE SYRIAN GREEKS

After a century of Ptolemaic Greek rule, the Jews had new masters, the Syrian-based Seleucid Greeks. In 200 BC, King Antiochus III gave the Jews a charter guaranteeing them religious freedom.

Secure in the belief that Antiochus's charter would protect their religion, many Jews copied other Greek customs. They wore Greek clothes, adopted Greek manners and gave their children Greek names.

Pro-Greek Jews were in favour of Greek education. At the *gymnasion* their sons studied Homer, Greek philosophy and music. These were taught in the Greek tradition of using questions and answers.

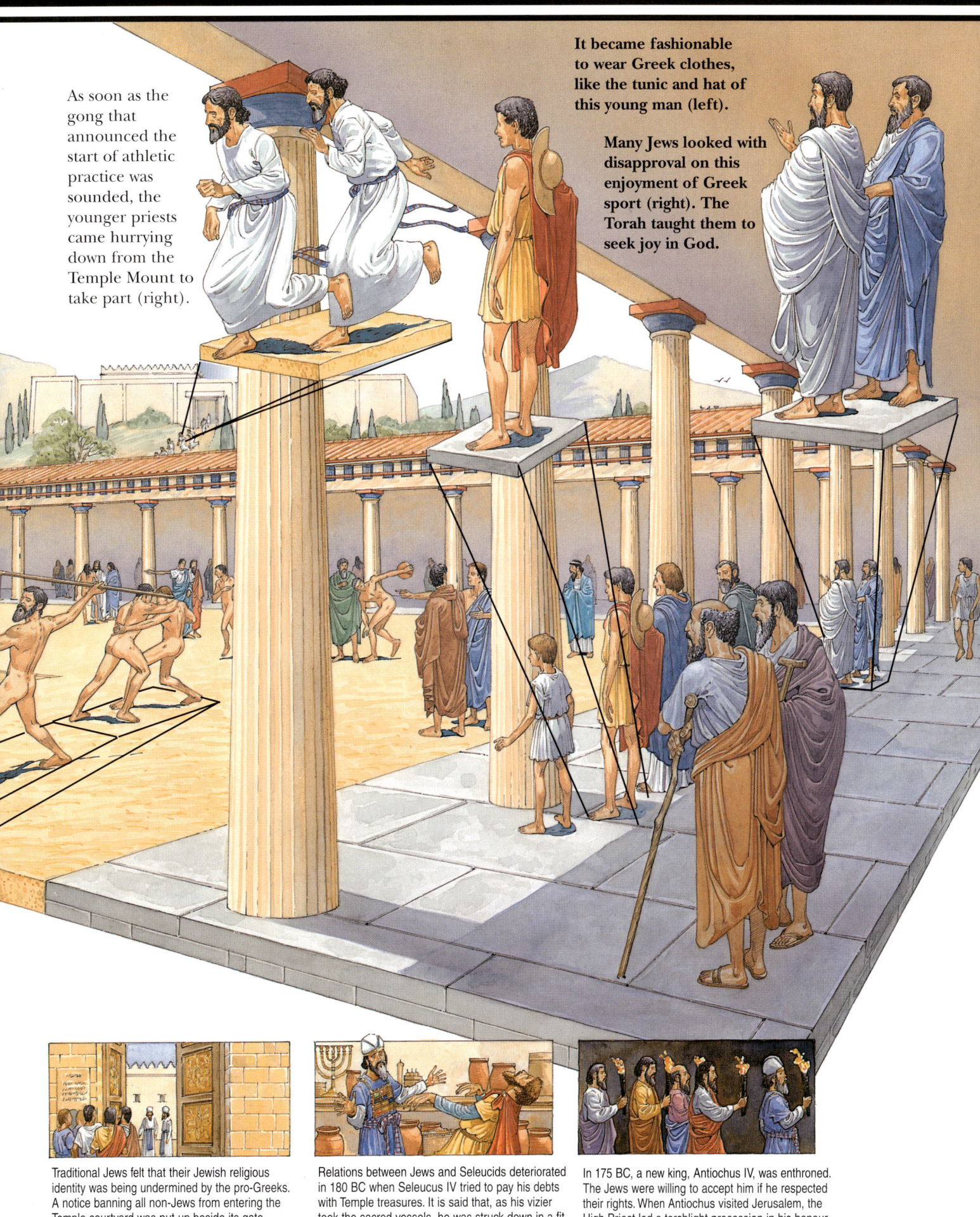

As soon as the gong that announced the start of athletic practice was sounded, the younger priests came hurrying down from the Temple Mount to take part (right).

It became fashionable to wear Greek clothes, like the tunic and hat of this young man (left).

Many Jews looked with disapproval on this enjoyment of Greek sport (right). The Torah taught them to seek joy in God.

Traditional Jews felt that their Jewish religious identity was being undermined by the pro-Greeks. A notice banning all non-Jews from entering the Temple courtyard was put up beside its gate.

Relations between Jews and Seleucids deteriorated in 180 BC when Seleucus IV tried to pay his debts with Temple treasures. It is said that, as his vizier took the sacred vessels, he was struck down in a fit.

In 175 BC, a new king, Antiochus IV, was enthroned. The Jews were willing to accept him if he respected their rights. When Antiochus visited Jerusalem, the High Priest led a torchlight procession in his honour.

ANTIOCHUS VIOLATES THE TEMPLE

REVOLT OF THE MACCABEES

AS LONG AS THEIR SELEUCID OVERLORDS did not interfere in religious matters, the Jews were content. However, any interference with the Temple aroused their fury. Antiochus IV miscalculated badly when he thought that, by forcing his subjects to share the same religion, he would unite them. He abolished the charter of religious tolerance and forced the Jews to worship Greek gods. Those who resisted were put to death. The leader who freed them from this tyranny was Judas Maccabeus (or Judas the Hammer – he and his four brothers are known as the Maccabees). He is a Jewish national hero.

Antiochus's need for money led him to give the post of Temple High Priest to candidates who offered bribes. He did this at least twice.

Antiochus's second appointee sold Temple treasures to pay the bribe he had promised. Angry Jews rioted in Jerusalem in protest.

Hearing that Antiochus had been killed in battle, the previous High Priest swept into Jerusalem with his supporters and his rival fled.

Antiochus, who was not dead, interpreted these disturbances as rebellion. His army stormed into Jerusalem and looted the Temple.

Antiochus IV (portrayed on a medal, below) had a troubled reign. His power was dwindling and was being challenged by many groups, including a new power – the Romans.

Medal portraying Antiochus IV

At the feast of Dionysus, a Greek god, dancing female revellers (above) approached the garlanded altar. Jews were forced to join in.

To people like priest Mattathias and his sons (right), drunken dancing on holy ground was an abomination.

JEWISH FAITH BANNED

Antiochus revoked his father's charter of 200 BC. Temple services were forbidden and sacred books were burned.

A 90-year-old man went to his death rather than eat pork. According to Jewish holy law, pigs are unclean animals.

Circumcision, a duty commanded in the Torah, was forbidden. Mothers who circumcised their sons were thrown from the walls.

Jews who were rounded up by Antiochus's men on the Sabbath would not fight back. They were all slaughtered.

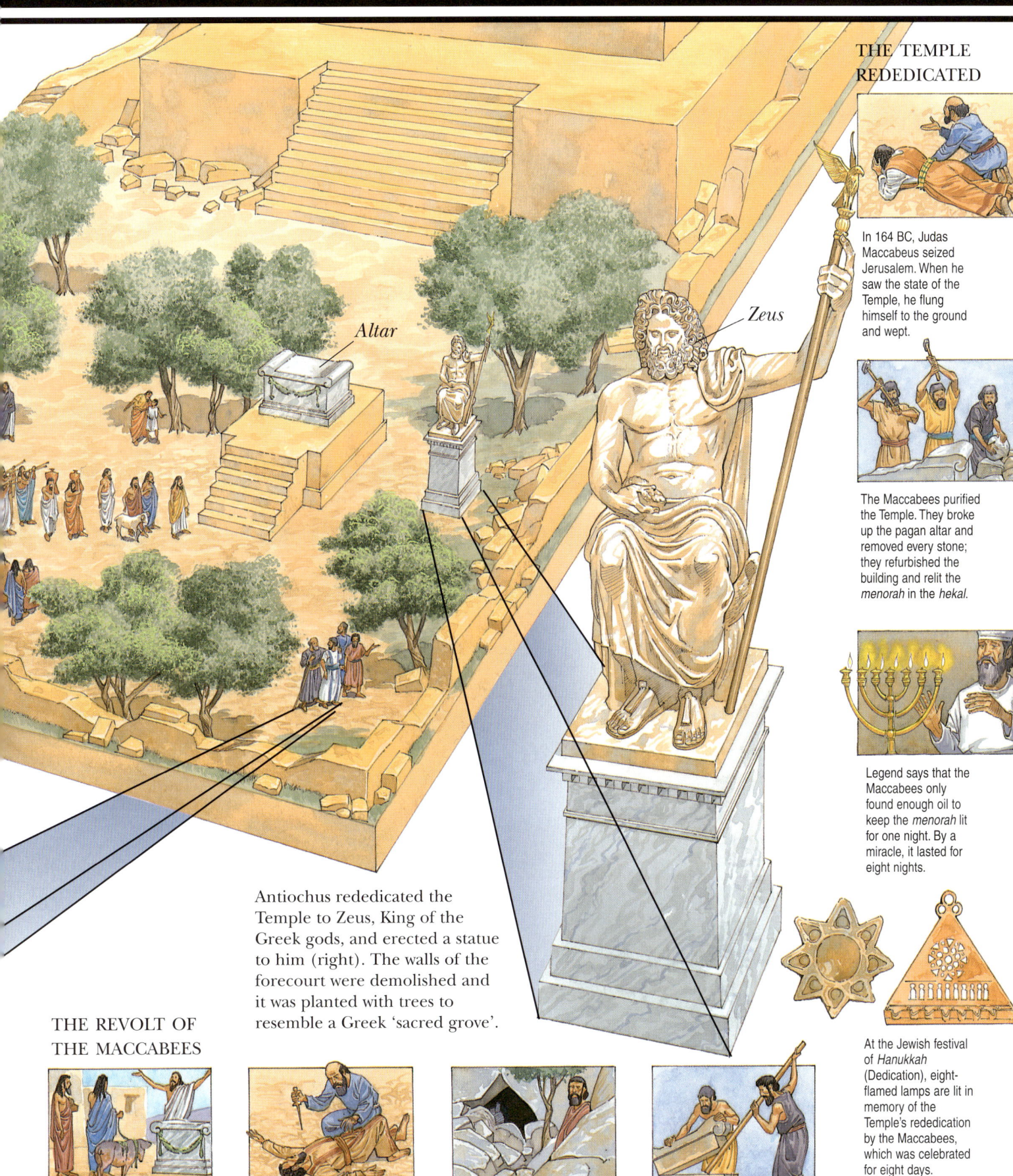

THE TEMPLE REDEDICATED

In 164 BC, Judas Maccabeus seized Jerusalem. When he saw the state of the Temple, he flung himself to the ground and wept.

The Maccabees purified the Temple. They broke up the pagan altar and removed every stone; they refurbished the building and relit the *menorah* in the *hekal*.

Legend says that the Maccabees only found enough oil to keep the *menorah* lit for one night. By a miracle, it lasted for eight nights.

At the Jewish festival of *Hanukkah* (Dedication), eight-flamed lamps are lit in memory of the Temple's rededication by the Maccabees, which was celebrated for eight days.

Antiochus rededicated the Temple to Zeus, King of the Greek gods, and erected a statue to him (right). The walls of the forecourt were demolished and it was planted with trees to resemble a Greek 'sacred grove'.

THE REVOLT OF THE MACCABEES

Soldiers forced the villagers of Judea to offer pagan sacrifices. When they reached the priest Mattathias' village he refused.

One of the villagers stepped forward to obey. At once Mattathias knifed him to death, as well as the commanding officer.

Mattathias and his five sons fled to the hills with other religious rebels. They formed a band of freedom-fighters.

When Mattathias died, his son Judas led the rebels. They overturned Greek altars, ambushed military patrols and spread revolt.

25

HASMONEAN PRIEST KINGS

Each Hasmonean ruler (Hasmon was the family name of the Maccabees) was both king and high priest. At first, the dynasty was popular.

People later began to think that this joint role gave the kings too much power. One king was pelted with fruit while serving in the Temple.

Two rival religious parties developed in Jerusalem. The Sadducees, the powerful priestly class, supported the rule of the priest-kings.

Their opponents, the Pharisees, did more work among the people. They opposed the Hasmoneans and stirred up revolt.

ROMAN JERUSALEM

From 164 BC to 63 BC, Judea was an independent state ruled by the Hasmoneans (descendants of the Maccabees). They made the country prosperous and enlarged its territory. In the meantime, the Romans were growing more powerful. When a power struggle split the Hasmonean family, the Romans seized their chance to take over Judea. The Jews were eventually given a king of Roman choosing – Herod the Great.

Roman soldiers

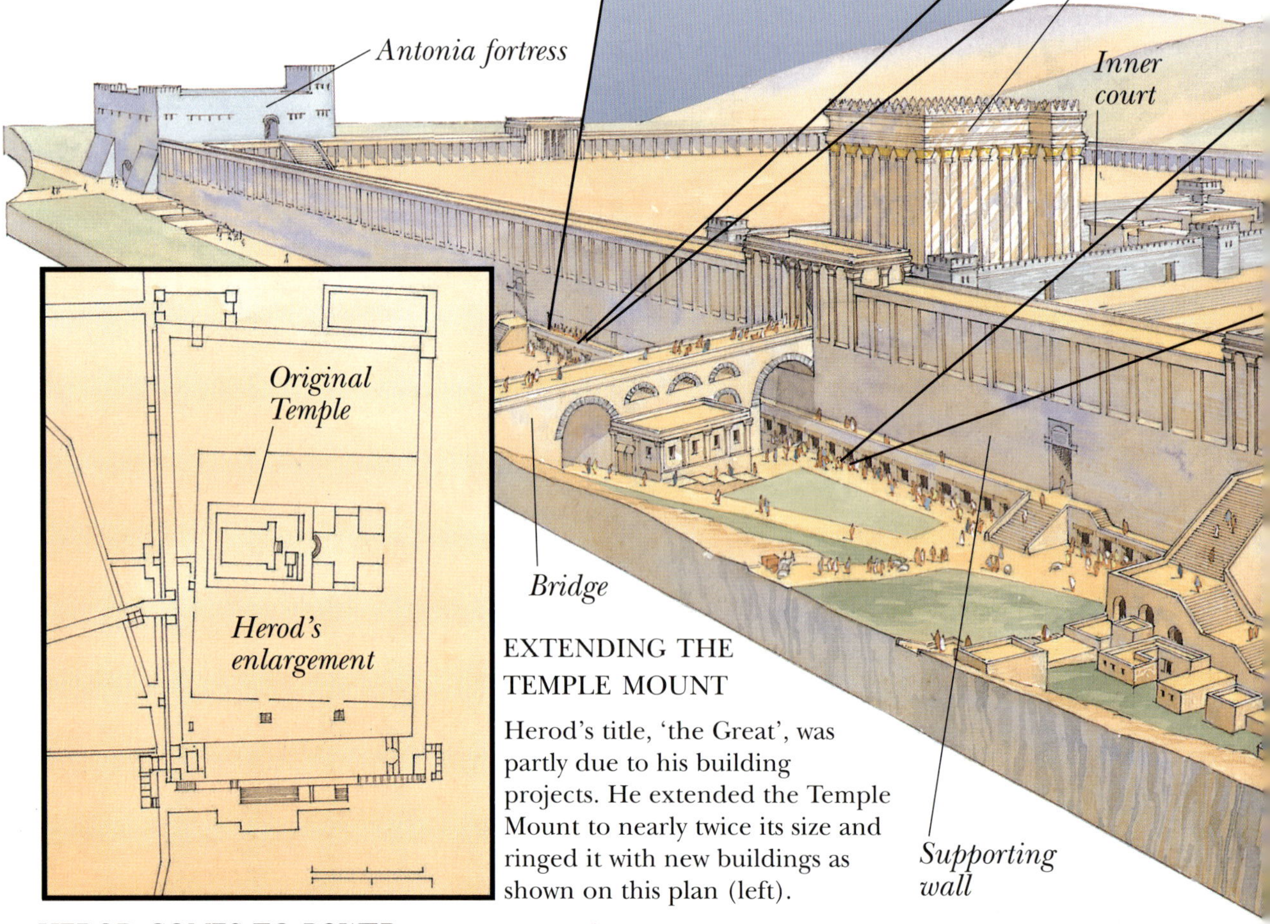

Antonia fortress

Temple

Inner court

Original Temple

Herod's enlargement

Bridge

Supporting wall

EXTENDING THE TEMPLE MOUNT

Herod's title, 'the Great', was partly due to his building projects. He extended the Temple Mount to nearly twice its size and ringed it with new buildings as shown on this plan (left).

HEROD COMES TO POWER

Sadducees and Pharisees took sides when rival Hasmonean brothers fought to be king. One brother shut himself in the Temple and burned the bridge leading to it.

The other brother asked the Romans to help. In 63 BC, led by their general Pompey, they entered Jerusalem, killing thousands.

To the horror of the Jews, Pompey then entered the Temple (from which all gentiles were banned) and gazed into the Holy of Holies.

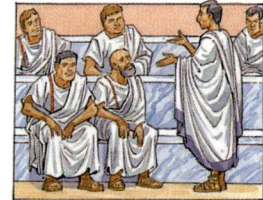

Soon after, an ambitious pro-Roman Jew called Herod fled to Rome and persuaded the Roman senate to make him king of Judea.

Roman soldiers, garrisoned in the new Antonia fortress, were a common sight in the streets of Jerusalem (left).

Shops at the foot of the supporting wall met the needs of pilgrims during their stay in the city (below).

Under the magnificent new portico, money changers (below) sold the special Temple coins without images, which had to be used in the Temple precinct.

Royal portico

Court of the Gentiles

Approach steps

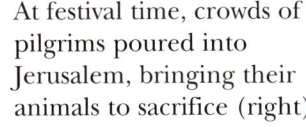

At festival time, crowds of pilgrims poured into Jerusalem, bringing their animals to sacrifice (right).

HEROD'S NEW JERUSALEM

Herod took Jerusalem by force, aided by Roman troops. He built a fortress near the Temple called the Antonia fortress.

He then set about transforming Jerusalem, redesigning the streets and building a palace for himself with water gardens.

Herod built a theatre and hippodrome in the upper city where games were held in honour of the Roman emperor.

He extended the Temple platform beyond its hilltop by supporting it on massive piers and vaults. This was a huge task, taking 80 years.

27

HEROD'S REFURBISHMENT

In a speech to the National Assembly, Herod assured the Jews that he meant to restore the Temple, not pull it down and start again.

The building materials were assembled before work began. More than 1,000 carts and wagons were needed to transport them.

Hundreds of priests were trained as carpenters and masons so that no person who was not a priest set foot inside the Temple.

Throughout the building work, sacrifices were offered as usual, so that the traditions of the Temple were unbroken.

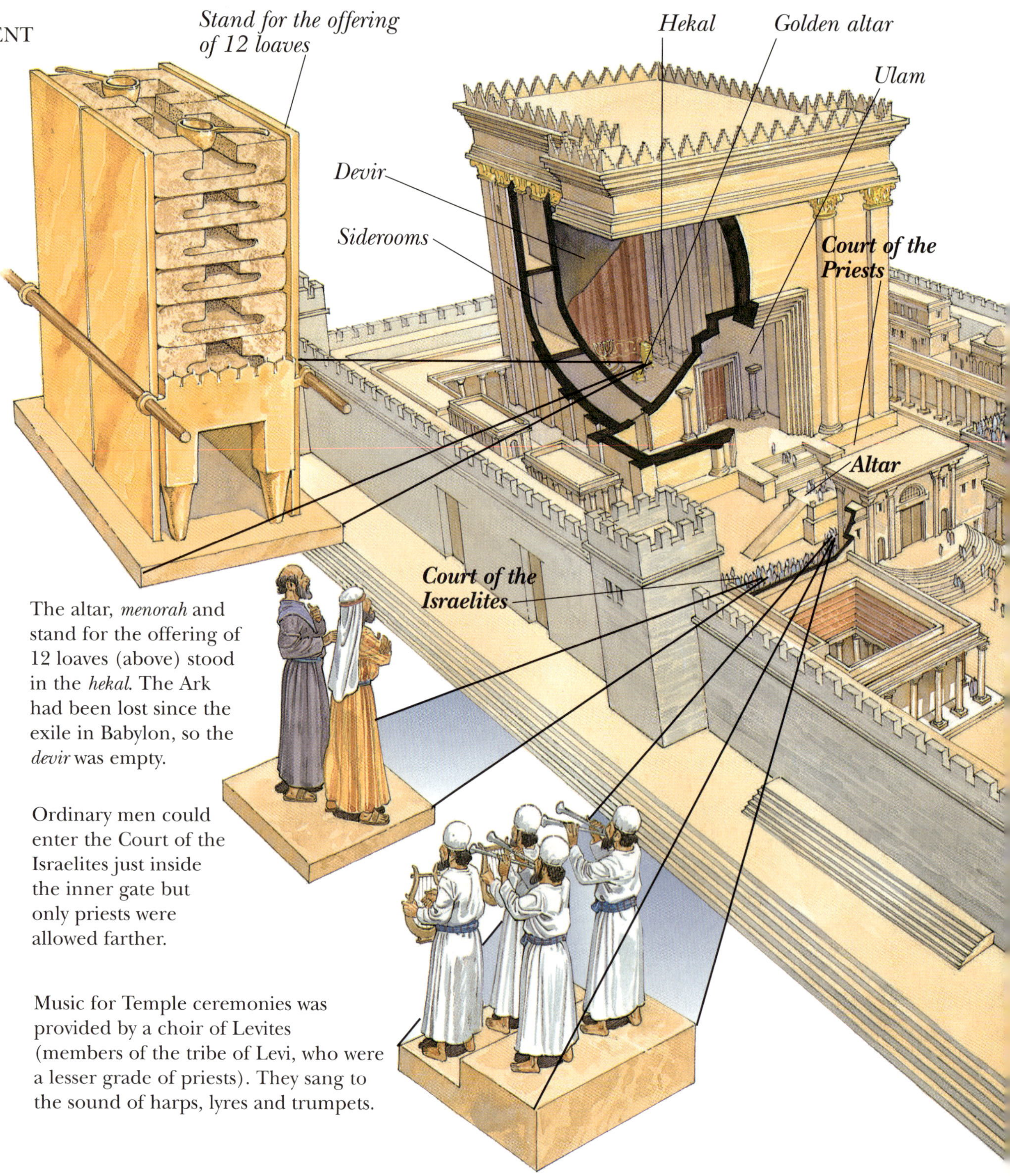

Stand for the offering of 12 loaves

Hekal

Golden altar

Devir

Ulam

Siderooms

Court of the Priests

Altar

Court of the Israelites

The altar, *menorah* and stand for the offering of 12 loaves (above) stood in the *hekal*. The Ark had been lost since the exile in Babylon, so the *devir* was empty.

Ordinary men could enter the Court of the Israelites just inside the inner gate but only priests were allowed farther.

Music for Temple ceremonies was provided by a choir of Levites (members of the tribe of Levi, who were a lesser grade of priests). They sang to the sound of harps, lyres and trumpets.

THE RITUAL OF SACRIFICE

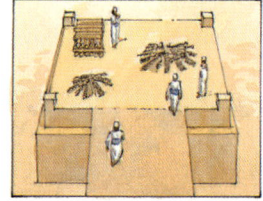

Three fires burned on the altar: one for sacrifices, one to provide hot coals for the altar in the *hekal*, and one that was not allowed to go out.

Certain priests selected live lambs from the store for sacrifice every day. All animals had to be free from disqualifying defects.

Each animal was killed according to rules written in the Torah. Its blood was collected in a cup and sprinkled on the altar base.

The various portions of sacrifice were brought to the altar, together with an offering of unleavened bread.

Herod's Temple

Women were only allowed in the first courtyard. They watched the sacrifices from the terraces there.

THE JUDEANS did not like Herod. He was cruel, tyrannical and foreign (he came from neighbouring Idumea). However, he was a clever ruler. He developed a plan that would both please his subjects and satisfy his own appetite for grand building projects – he would lavishly restore the Temple. Work on the Temple itself, begun in 20 BC, was finished in 18 months, but its surroundings took 46 years to complete. Herod did not live to see the Temple Mount in its final glory, with its vast courts and porticoes, its marble-clad walls and its gilded pilasters gleaming in the sun.

Court of the Women

PROBABLE PLAN OF THE TEMPLE
1. Court of the Israelites
2. Court of the Priests
3. Altar of Burnt Offerings
4. Ritual slaughter area
5. Temple proper
6. Court of the Women

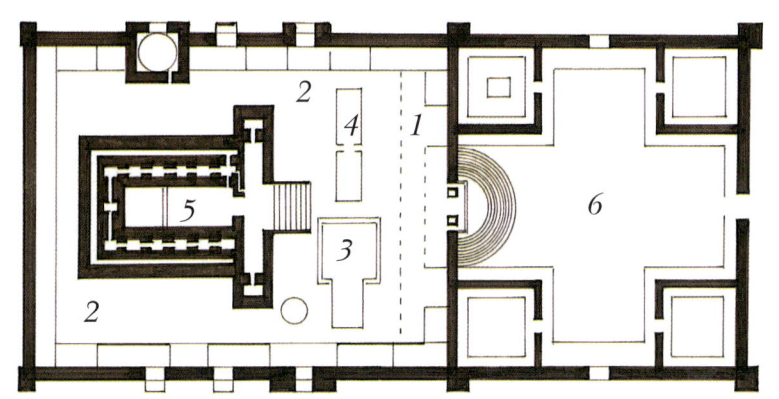

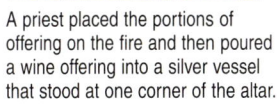

A priest placed the portions of offering on the fire and then poured a wine offering into a silver vessel that stood at one corner of the altar.

The priest who was overseeing the ceremonies then gave the sign for the choir of Levites to sound their trumpets and begin the daily song.

A signal indicated that priests in the *hekal* were offering incense. As they threw themselves down in worship, everyone outside did too.

Priests then gave a blessing: "The Lord bless you and keep you,...the Lord lift up his countenance upon you and give you peace."

RITUAL PURITY

Worshippers first had to be 'purified' by taking a ritual bath. Some baths had two doors, so that those going in did not pollute those coming out.

Before performing any part of the sacrificial service a priest had to wash his hands and feet at a ewer beside the Temple door.

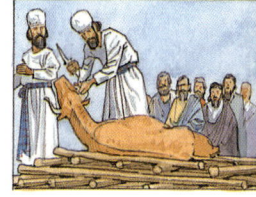

Some things, such as contact with death, made people so 'impure' that they could only be cleansed through the sacrifice of a red heifer.

At a special ceremony, the ashes of the heifer were mingled with water and sprinkled with a hyssop sprig upon the 'impure' person.

APPOINTING THE PRIESTS

On his appointment, the High Priest had to swear an oath to the Sanhedrin (the Jewish law-making assembly) that he would faithfully follow the Torah.

Candidates for the priesthood were closely questioned by the Sanhedrin to ensure they had no faults that made them unsuitable.

The priests were split into 24 shifts, each of which served for a week. Each shift was made up of 6 family clans, each serving for one day of the week and all serving on the Sabbath.

On a new priest's first day of serving in the Temple, he brought his own special offering of 12 small loaves to the altar.

PRIESTS AND LEVITES

ACCORDING TO JEWISH TRADITION, the vestments worn by Temple priests were of the same design and materials as those that God had ordered Moses to make for the tabernacle. The High Priest wore the eight 'golden garments': short trousers, tunic, robe, *ephod*, breastplate, girdle, turban and forehead-plate. The girdle and the richly patterned *ephod* were woven of blue, purple and crimson wools intertwined with gold thread. Ordinary priests wore a simple tunic, turban and girdle. Priests wore nothing on their feet in order not to pollute the holy ground of the Temple and its courts.

Turban
Girdle

Ordinary priests wore a white linen tunic, a patterned girdle and a plain white turban (left).

Temple

On the Day of Atonement (see pages 32-33) the High Priest wore his 'white garments': a simple tunic, turban and girdle (left).

High Priest

THE PRIESTS' DAY

On the night before his day of duty, a priest slept on the floor in the 'Place of Fire', the kitchen-dormitory of the Temple.

Before dawn, the day's tasks were allotted by counting around the group as each man held out a finger to be counted.

At dawn, two patrols went in opposite directions around the Temple courts. When they met they exchanged the greeting, "Peace."

Priests preparing the main altar added new logs and removed the ash of the previous day with a silver shovel.

Forehead-plate

Breastplate

The breastplate held 12 gemstones inscribed with the names of Israel's tribes.

THE LEVITES

The Levites provided the music for the morning and evening services and sang a different psalm for each day.

The gold forehead-plate (above) was inscribed with the words "Holy to God."

Turban

The short trousers (below), worn by all priests, had no front opening, as 'unclean' bodily functions were never performed while they were being worn.

Ephod

Girdle

The *ephod*, a richly embroidered garment, is not clearly described in the Bible. The traditional Jewish version of it is pictured left. On the right is a costume historian's version.

Ephod

Robe

Tunic

Triple crown

According to an eye-witness at the time of Herod's temple, the High Priest wore a triple crown (above).

The Levites were the Temple's guardians, keeping watch at 21 points around the Temple courts and at the five gates leading into the Temple Mount.

A Levite signalled the beginning and the end of the Sabbath by blowing a silver trumpet from the walls of the Temple Mount.

The Levites were also responsible for unlocking the Temple doors at the start of morning service and closing them at the end of the day.

High Priest – traditional Jewish version

High Priest – costume historian's version

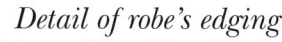

Detail of robe's edging

A priest prepared the golden altar by sweeping its ash into a gold jar. Another cleaned the oil cups of the *menorah* and renewed their wicks.

When everything was ready, the priests reassembled for a period of prayer and meditation before the daily sacrifice.

A priest was chosen only once in his lifetime to offer incense in the *hekal*. He cast the incense onto the altar fire with his bare hands.

At the end of the day, the priests assembled in the Place of Fire to eat some parts of the sacrifice that were not offered on the altar.

PREPARING FOR THE CEREMONY

For the week before *Yom Kippur*, the High Priest withdrew to his room in the Temple to prepare himself mentally for the sacred tasks of the day.

On the day before the festival, the sacrificial animals were led before the High Priest who scrutinised each creature for defects.

The High Priest stayed awake for the entire night before the day itself. He discussed the Torah or was read to, so that he didn't fall asleep.

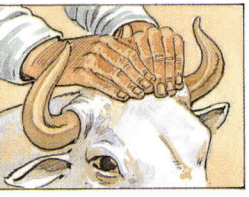

The next day, in front of the Temple, the High Priest asked first to be forgiven for his own sins, laying his hands on the head of a sacrificial bullock.

THE DAY OF ATONEMENT

THE MOST SOLEMN and dramatic of the Temple's festival days was the Day of Atonement (*Yom Kippur*). The Jews were very aware of a duty to act correctly, which for them meant obeying God's Law, as revealed in the Torah. To do otherwise was sinful. They also understood that human beings are far from perfect and that to obey all the time was sometimes difficult. Through the ceremony of *Yom Kippur* they begged God to wipe out their past sins and let them start with a clean slate. Their sins were symbolically transferred to a sacrificial goat which was cast from a cliff, taking the sins with it.

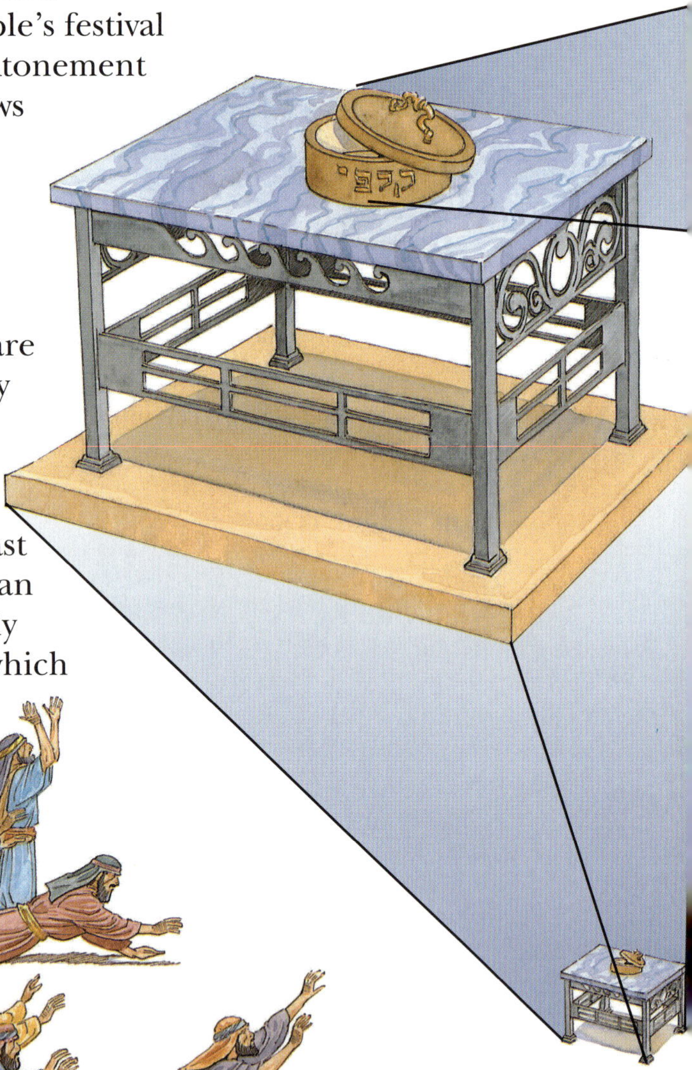

THE CEREMONIES OF ATONEMENT

Two goats played vital roles in the festival of Atonement. One was to be sacrificed on the altar of burnt offerings; the other would become the 'scapegoat' who carried away the people's sins. With much prayer and ceremony, the High Priest drew lots to discover which role each goat was destined to play.

On this day of the year only, the High Priest entered the Holy of Holies. He set a golden shovel of hot coals on the Foundation Stone and burned incense in it.

Wooden lottery box

The High Priest's assistants handed him two lengths of crimson wool (right). He tied one around the neck of the sacrifice and the other round the horns of the scapegoat.

The High Priest took two lots (right) from a lottery box (above) and, without looking at them, put one on the head of each goat. The lot marked "For the Lord" denoted the sacrifice; the other denoted the scapegoat.

Placing the lots on the goats, the High Priest recited the Holy Name of God. At the sound of this word, all the people bowed to the ground.

The High Priest then returned to the scapegoat. Laying his hands on its head, he begged God to forgive the Jews' sins and to set them on the goat.

The High Priest then entrusted the scapegoat to the priest who had been chosen to lead it, with its invisible burden of sins, out of Jerusalem and into the desert. He lead the animal garlanded with crimson wool out of the eastern gate of the Temple Mount, where many people gathered to watch its departure.

THE FATE OF THE SCAPEGOAT

Booths were set up along the priest's route in the desert. The attendant at each booth accompanied him to the next one on the route.

By a cliff in a remote desert region, the priest took wool from the goat's horns and tied some of it to a rock. He then pushed the animal over the cliff.

The crimson wool changed to white, as a sign that the sins were forgiven. The news was sent to Jerusalem by waving a cloth from booth to booth.

The High Priest then read aloud a passage from the biblical book of Leviticus. In the passage, God tells Moses how *Yom Kippur* is to be celebrated.

33

MAKING THE PILGRIMAGE

Pilgrimages gave people the chance to take a holiday. Farmers and their families came from afar, often in organised parties with a group leader.

During the long journey to Jerusalem, the pilgrims would eat and drink together at night, joke, laugh and sing popular songs.

In Jerusalem, officials made arrangements for the pilgrims. They inspected wells and public baths and found accommodation in private houses.

Pilgrims who could not be put up in Jerusalem camped outside. During Herod's reign, up to 500,000 pilgrims were in the city at festival time.

Pilgrimage Festivals

THE THREE major pilgrimage festivals, Passover, *Shavuot* and *Sukkot* were originally agricultural festivals. Passover had marked the coming of spring; *Shavuot*, in early summer, was the Feast of the First Fruits, and *Sukkot* was a harvest festival. The Israelites gave the festivals new, historical meanings. Passover commemorated their escape from Egypt, *Shavuot*, Moses' receiving of the Law, and *Sukkot*, the Israelites' wanderings in the desert.

As pilgrims neared Jerusalem for the festival of *Shavuot*, they led an ox whose horns were overlaid with gold (below). They sang together, "I was glad when they said unto me, let us go unto the house of the Lord."

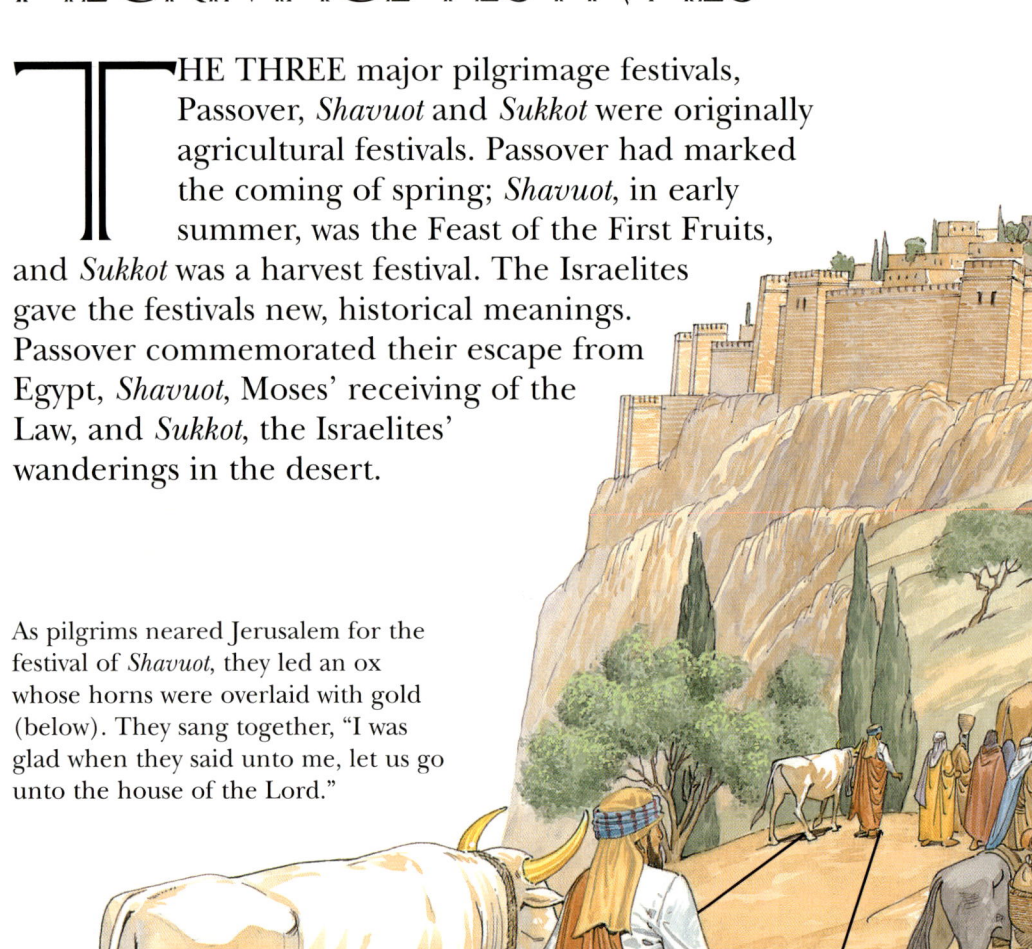

PASSOVER

The Passover commemorates the escape of the Israelites from Egypt, when God had commanded them to mark their door posts with the blood of a sacrificed lamb.

Each group of pilgrims brought a Passover offering of a lamb into the Temple court. This was the only time that ordinary people helped in the sacrifice.

After their lamb's blood had been sprinkled on the altar, people took its meat to be cooked in one of the special ovens set up throughout the city.

Each family or group then celebrated its *seder* or Passover thanksgiving supper, which was eaten reclining on cushions, as a sign of freedom.

The 'first fruits' that were brought to the Temple for *Shavuot* were of the seven kinds for which Israel was famous: wheat, barley, grapes, pomegranates, figs, olives and dates.

SUKKOT

At *Sukkot*, people brought leafy branches to Jerusalem, in order to make temporary huts. They lived in these for the week of the festival.

Every day, worshippers placed very long willow branches around the altar, so that they bent over the top of it.

Pilgrims brought the 'four species' to be blessed. These were sprays of myrtle, palm and willow held in the right hand, and a citron held in the left.

Each day at dawn, a water libation was performed. Priests filled a golden vessel from a spring outside the city and poured its water on the altar.

SHAVUOT

To ensure that the fruit offerings for *Shavuot* were truly the first of the year, farmers would mark the first fruit to ripen by tying a reed round it.

The ox with the gilded horns was a special sacrifice for the festival. Its arrival in Jerusalem was greeted by enthusiastic crowds, dancing and singing.

Each pilgrim brought his offering of first fruits in a round basket, presented it to a priest in the Temple courtyard and recited a special prayer after him.

The priest took the basket and raised it up in his hands as an offering to God. The pilgrim prostrated himself before the Temple as this was done.

35

TOPPLING THE EAGLE

In 4 BC, King Herod outraged the Jews by putting a gold eagle (symbol of Rome) above the Temple gate.

Hearing that the king was dead, students descended by rope to dislodge the eagle and hacked it to pieces.

Herod was ill but not yet dead. He summoned the leading citizens and told them of his fury.

Herod had the students and two teachers burnt alive. His death a few days later was seen as punishment for this.

In the reign of Herod's son, there were riots in Jerusalem. Roman troops were sent to restore order and crucified 2,000 Jews.

Titus, a Roman general, had offered to spare the Temple if the Jews surrendered. However, his men, impatient for looting, responded eagerly to their centurion's urging (right).

Roman centurion

THE JEWS IN REVOLT

In AD 26, Jews protested angrily when Roman standards with the Emperor's portrait were set up near the Temple.

Judea, now under direct Roman rule, was full of unrest. Suspect people, like Jesus of Nazareth, were put to death.

In AD 64, the Roman governor took Temple funds as tax arrears. Protesters pretended to beg for the 'hard up' governor.

Furious at this insult, the governor marched into Jerusalem with his troops. In the rioting that followed, the market place was destroyed.

Simon ben Giora

The Final Destruction

BARELY 35 YEARS after Herod's great project was completed, the Temple was destroyed. It caught fire as Jewish patriotic extremists called Zealots fought to defend it from the Romans. It might have been saved if the Zealots had compromised, but relationships between Jews and Romans had deteriorated rapidly since Herod's time. Four legions of the Roman army had been sent to put down the unrest in Judea, which was now under direct Roman rule. Yet even after months of siege, the Zealots urged the starving people of Jerusalem not to surrender but to die fighting for their right to live and worship as they wished.

Encouraged by their fanatical leader, Simon ben Giora (left), the Zealots fought every inch of the way. They did not despair until they saw the sanctuary itself in flames.

General Titus's victory over the Jews in AD 70 was celebrated in Rome by the erection of a triumphal arch. A detail from its reliefs (below) shows Roman soldiers parading the *menorah* and other Temple treasures through the streets of Rome.

THE TEMPLE DESTROYED

A Zealot suicide squad went out among the besiegers, flinging blazing torches that set the battering rams alight.

Titus had to change tactics. Blocking access to the city by surrounding it with a siege wall, he planned to starve it into surrender.

Still the Jews did not give in. Then, the Romans gained the Antonia fortress. From there they launched rocks and other weapons into the Temple.

On 28th August AD 70, the Romans gained the inner court. Jews cried out in horror as a soldier threw a firebrand into the Temple.

The Temple went up in flames and was reduced to rubble. Only part of the wall remained.

ROME SENDS ITS ARMY

In AD 66, Jewish Zealots gained control of Jerusalem. The Roman general Vespasian was sent with a large army to quell the revolt.

Vespasian planned to subdue Judea first, to isolate Jerusalem. Refugees fled as the Roman legions marched through the land.

In AD 69, Vespasian returned to Rome as Emperor and his son Titus took over. From a camp above Jerusalem, he planned his strategy.

Ramps of earth and timber were built to bring wooden towers with battering rams up to Jerusalem's three lines of walls.

THE RISE OF CHRISTIANITY

After the Temple

IN THE 2ND CENTURY AD, the Romans destroyed all that remained of Jerusalem and banned Jews from the site. Many were sold as slaves or fled abroad in the scattering of the Jews known as the Diaspora. By the 4th century, when Christianity was made the official Roman religion, a rebuilt Jerusalem had become a magnet for Christian pilgrims to the Holy Land. In the 7th century, when the Muslims captured it, Jerusalem became an Islamic holy city too. The Crusades were fought, unsuccessfully in the long run, to make it Christian again.

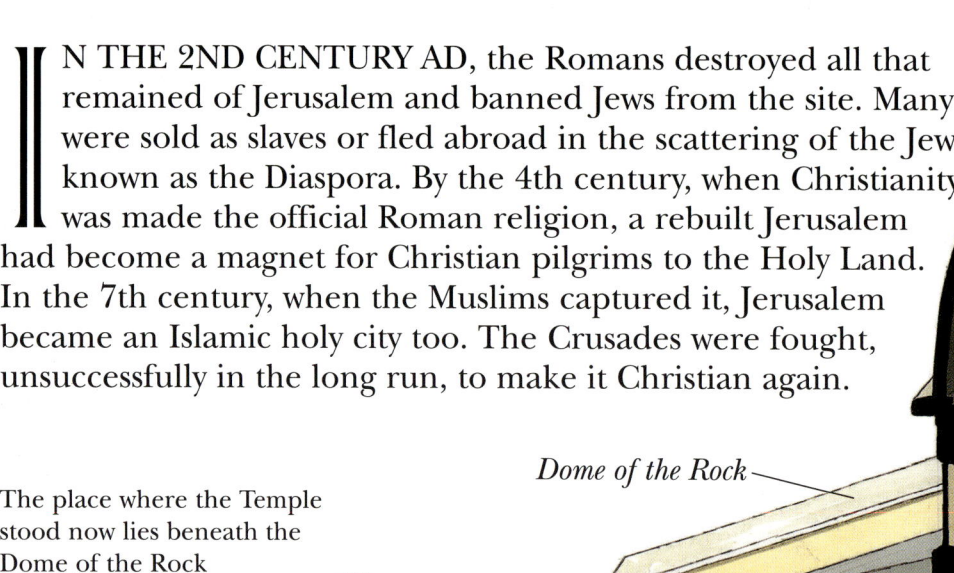

Dome of the Rock

In AD 132 a new Jewish revolt was sparked by Emperor Hadrian's decision to destroy Jerusalem. Every building was swept away and the site was levelled.

On the site of Jerusalem, Hadrian built a Roman city called *Aelia Capitolina*. The Temple platform was adorned with a statue of the Emperor.

In the 4th century AD, Emperor Constantine, a Christian convert, restored the name Jerusalem. Christ's burial place was excavated and the Church of the Holy Sepulchre built over it.

Christian pilgrims began to flood to Jerusalem to see the tomb of Christ and churches rose all over the city. Jerusalem became a Christian city in which Jews were second-class citizens.

The place where the Temple stood now lies beneath the Dome of the Rock (right), the Islamic mosque Caliph Abdel Malik built in AD 687. The rock it encloses may have been the site of the *devir*.

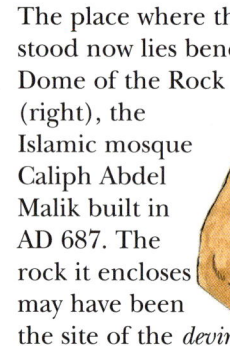

Without the Temple, the Jews centred their religious life on meeting halls called synagogues, in which they gathered to pray and study the Torah. Above, a mosaic from a synagogue of the 3rd-4th century AD. It shows a scene from the life of Abraham.

THE COMING OF ISLAM

In the 7th century AD, the Arab prophet Mohammed taught a new faith – Islam. Its followers are called Muslims.

When the Muslim Caliph Omar captured Jerusalem in AD 638, he entered the city on foot out of respect for its sacred past.

Caliph Omar was so disgusted to find the Temple site covered in refuse that he collected some and threw it over the walls.

Omar built a simple mosque on the Temple site. A later caliph, Abdel Malik, replaced this with the dazzling Dome of the Rock.

A section of an interior mosaic

The designs of the mosque's interior mosaics (left) show only scrolling plants. Like the Jews, the Muslims did not portray God.

Suleiman the Magnificent restored the Dome of the Rock in 1545. He replaced its damaged exterior mosaics with multi-coloured tiles (below left) and clad the lower walls in marble.

RETURN TO ISLAM

The victorious Crusaders turned the Dome of the Rock into a church and replaced its golden crescent, the symbol of Islam, with a cross.

An exterior multi-coloured tile

There are many legends about the rock inside the Dome. It came to be regarded as the spot from which Mohammed rose up to heaven. He had a vision that he had been borne through the night sky to Jerusalem from Mecca by his horse Burak. The 16th-century Persian painting below depicts this vision.

The Crusaders' triumph was shortlived. In 1187 they were defeated by the brilliant leader Saladin who reinstated Islam in Jerusalem.

Jerusalem enjoyed a period of glory under Suleiman the Magnificent in the 16th century, but the next three centuries saw its slow decline.

Islamic rule in Jerusalem did not officially end until 1922 when the League of Nations gave Britain the mandate to govern Jerusalem.

16th-century Persian painting

CRUSADES IN JERUSALEM

Early Muslim rulers were tolerant of Jews. While praying on the Mount of Olives, Jews could gaze on the Temple site.

Islamic tolerance of Jews and Christians ended in the 11th century when the fierce Seljuk Turks seized power.

Christians vowed to regain their Holy Land from the Muslims. In 1095, Pope Urban II launched a 'holy war', the First Crusade.

In 1099, the Crusader forces broke into Jerusalem, killing an estimated 40,000 people and looting the Dome of the Rock.

THE JEWS RETURN

In 1897, the first Zionist Conference proposed this Star of David as the emblem of the new Jewish state it hoped to found in Palestine.

The Zionist movement encouraged Jews throughout Europe to buy land in Palestine and settle there to form farming communities.

The Jewish national flag was unfurled in 1948 as the existence of the independent Jewish state of Israel was proclaimed.

Jews and Arabs now live together in Jerusalem. The belief of each that the city is theirs by right has led to disputes that are still unsettled.

THE TEMPLE SITE TODAY

TODAY THE TOP OF THE TEMPLE MOUNT is the Muslims' *Haram ash-Sharif* (Noble Sanctuary). Orthodox Jews will not set foot on it for fear they might unknowingly tread where their Holy of Holies had been. All that remains of the Jewish Temple is a stretch of the wall that Herod built to support his extension of the Mount. Known as the Western Wall, or the Wailing Wall, it is for Jews the most holy place in Jerusalem. They believe that the *Sheshina* (the Presence of God) would never forsake any part of the Temple and is still present in the stones of the wall. Today, the area in front of the wall serves as a kind of an open-air synagogue where Jews from all over the world come to pray and to lament the loss of their Temple.

PILGRIMS AND PRAYER

From medieval times, Palestine's Islamic rulers had permitted the few remaining Jews to live in Jerusalem once again. They were allowed to pray at the Western Wall, but houses had been built so close to the wall that only a narrow, cramped alley remained. The houses were cleared away in 1976.

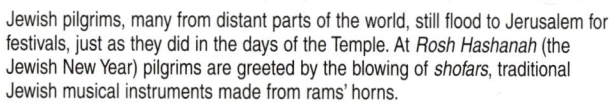

Jewish pilgrims, many from distant parts of the world, still flood to Jerusalem for festivals, just as they did in the days of the Temple. At *Rosh Hashanah* (the Jewish New Year) pilgrims are greeted by the blowing of *shofars*, traditional Jewish musical instruments made from rams' horns.

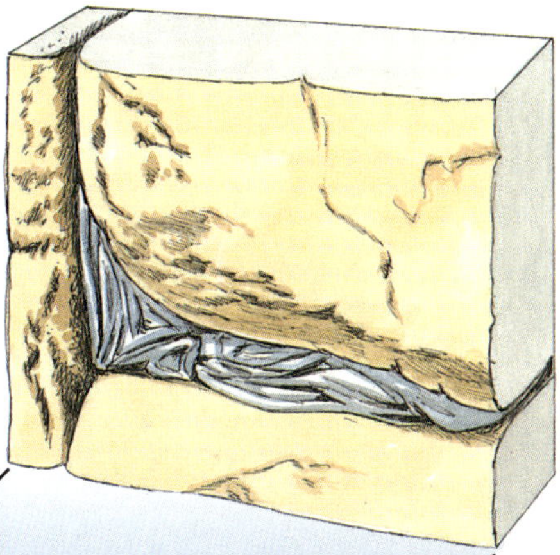

CITY OF THREE FAITHS

A low screen divides the pavement just in front of the Wall into an area for women and a larger one for men. Here Orthodox Jewish men, wearing hats and traditional black clothes (right), break off their prayers from time to time to kiss the stones of the Wall.

Many people write prayers on paper which they thrust into cracks in the Wall (left), hoping that this will ensure an answer.

Torah scroll

A Torah scroll (above) contains the first 5 books of the Bible, containing the commandments that rule Jewish religious life. Its text is handwritten in Hebrew with a quill pen. Each synagogue has its own Torah scroll.

These Roman Catholic Franciscan friars, like all Christian pilgrims to Jerusalem, are following the route along which Jesus carried his cross.

Two Muslims kiss hands in a traditional greeting. Muslims honour Abraham and Jesus of Nazareth as forerunners of Mohammed.

A Greek Orthodox priest at the Church of the Holy Sepulchre. Various Christian denominations share responsibility for the Christian holy sites.

A Jew at prayer covers his head with a *tallith* (prayer shawl). *Tefillin* (small boxes holding holy texts) are bound to his forehead and left arm.

The Jewish ceremony of the 'Rejoicing of the Torah', on the last day of *Sukkot*, commemorates the completion of the year's readings from the Torah. In each synagogue, the Torah scroll is taken from its ark and carried under a bridal canopy to the Western Wall, followed by a procession of worshippers.

Jerusalem is Islam's third most holy city after Mecca, Mohammed's birth place and Medina, where he preached. The platform of the Temple Mount is now an Islamic sacred area, where huge crowds of Muslims assemble every Friday to pray in the open air, bowing towards the Al-Aqsa mosque.

Timespan

c. 2000-1200 BC It is only possible to give very approximate dates for the earliest stories in Jewish history. Abraham is revered as a historical person by devout Jews, Christians, and Muslims. However, some scholars regard him as a legendary figure who represents a migratory shepherd tribe in the earliest stage of its history. The biblical account of Abraham leaving the city of Ur to settle in Canaan may be connected with the sack of Ur by raiders in 1960 BC.

The story of Joseph is also hard to date. The Bible does not name the pharaoh whom Joseph served, or the pharaoh who would not let Moses and his people leave Egypt about four centuries later. However, it is probable that this second pharaoh is Rameses II. This would date the escape of the Israelites from Egypt to c. 1250 BC and their arrival in Canaan to c. 1200 BC.

c. 1020 BC Saul is anointed the Israelites' first king.

c. 1000 BC King David captures the Jebusite stronghold of Jerusalem and transforms it into his capital. He installs the Ark of the Covenant there.

c. 950 BC King Solomon builds the first Temple to house the Ark.

c. 922 BC On the death of Solomon his realm is split into two kingdoms, Israel and Judah.

722 BC Israel is destroyed by the Assyrians and its people deported.

597 BC Judah falls to the the Babylonians.

586 BC The Babylonians besiege Jerusalem, destroy the Temple, and take the Jews captive to Babylon.

The menorah

539 BC The Babylonian Empire falls to King Cyrus of Persia who allows the Jews to return to Jerusalem. Some choose to stay in Babylon where they form a community that has remained until modern times.

520 BC The foundations of the Second Temple are laid.

515 BC The Temple is rebuilt. In the Second Temple, the Holy of Holies is empty. After the Babylonian destruction of the first Temple, nothing more was heard of the Ark. Its fate is a mystery. It is not listed among the Temple treasures restored to the Jews by the Persians. There is a Jewish tradition stating that it was smuggled out of Jerusalem by the prophet Jeremiah, in order to preserve it from the Babylonians, and that the knowledge of its hiding place was somehow lost.

Little is known of the Temple's history while Jerusalem was under Persian rule.

333 BC Alexander the Great defeats the Persians. After his death, Jerusalem eventually falls under the rule of the Seleucid dynasty in Syria.

c. 168 BC The Seleucid King Antiochus IV outlaws the Jewish faith and puts its followers to death.

Golden cherubim